CW01261768

The North-West Devon Coast:
A Celebration of Cliffs and Seashore from the Hartland Peninsula to the Taw-Torridge Estuary.
First published by **Thematic Trails** in paperback (October 2013) ISBN 978-0-948444-61-6.
This hardback edition, with a sewn-binding and minor text and lay-out changes,
was published in July 2014.   ISBN 978-0-948444-65-4   © Peter Keene 2014

Thematic Trails
7 Norwood Avenue, Kingston Bagpuize. Oxfordshire. OX13 5AD   www.thematic-trails.org

Printed by Berforts Information Press, Eynsham, Oxfordshire. U.K.

All photography by Peter Keene unless otherwise stated in the Acknowledgements.
Editorial advice and copy editing by Janet Keene. Design, layout and editing by Peter Keene.

This book is dedicated to my parents for a natural Westward Ho! childhood

Bideford Bay from Kipling Tors, Westward Ho!

Safety: *In this book I have spoken of the joy of exploring remote coves and beaches by kayak. It should be emphasised that such sea kayaking is not undertaken lightly. Strong tidal currents and rapidly changing sea conditions can make this a hazardous adventure if undertaken by those with little experience of sea kayaking. The best place to learn is a sandy, sheltered beach where after an upset you at least stand a chance of being washed ashore in one piece.*

If you venture down onto cliff-backed beaches be aware that the tidal range here is large. keep an eye open for a rising tide. High tides often reach the cliff foot and can trap the unwary. Rogue waves are also a danger. Avoid standing immediately below steep, rocky sea cliffs which can shed loose blocks of rock without warning. This is the site of nature in action.

All rights reserved. No part of this book may be reprinted or reproduced or utilised in any form or by any electronic, mechanical or other means, now known or hereafter invented, including photocopying and recording, or any other information storage or retrieval system, without the permission in writing from the publishers.

Front cover photo: Hartland Quay with cliffs.
Frontispiece photo: Crow Point and the Taw-Torridge estuary with Appledore and Instow.
Contents page photos: Milford Common. Smoothlands. Clovelly. Westward Ho! ridge cusps.
Rear cover: Map of the North-West Devon coast with places mentioned in the text.

The North-West Devon Coast

A Celebration of Cliffs and Seashore

from the Hartland Peninsula to the Taw-Torridge Estuary

Information for the reader

Most of the Thematic Trails I have written, edited or published have essentially been about 'explanation' of landscapes in one form or another. This book is rather different, more a 'celebration' of scenery and in particular the coastal environment of North-West Devon, treating the landscapes more as experiences of place and poetry of shape, rather than analysis and evolution of landforms.

The book began one calm midsummer evening in 2009 when a good friend of mine, Kester Webb of Exmoor, arranged a photographic flight for me in a light aircraft. My pilot met the coast at the Cornish border and, flying at clifftop level along the Hartland Heritage Coast, we swung around Hartland Point and hugged the cliffs of Bideford Bay until we reached the Taw-Torridge estuary. From low over the Atlantic and from a clear sky, the sun bathed the cliffs in a soft, evening light. Unused to private flights in small aircraft, the flight was a moving experience for me. On a coast I thought I knew so well, the different perspective made this a stunning voyage of discovery.

> *"The real act of discovery consists not in finding new lands, but in seeing with new eyes."*
> (Marcel Proust).

The core of this book consists of a selection of landscape photos I took that day. The air photos are displayed in chronological order, from the Cornish border to Appledore on the Taw-Torridge estuary. Most of these photos are displayed as full-page landscapes on left-hand (even-numbered) pages. These, I think, form a remarkable record of this spectacular landscape. Some readers may simply wish to allow these landscapes to speak for themselves.

However, each landscape photo is linked (on the facing page) with a commentary, consisting of photos, artwork and sometimes explanations and quotations by others who have written about these locations. The commentary is also interlaced with my own personal experience of this coast for which I have a long-standing emotional attachment, not least for its beauty and grandeur.

Being brought up in Westward Ho! I began exploring and familiarising myself with this coast at an early age, first by walking, then cycling and later by kayak, from which I was able to land in inaccessible coves and beaches, recording what I found both with photos and by writing logs and keeping a Commonplace Book. After taking a Geography degree at Hull University, my career took me away from my home village to teach in London but within two years I was bringing students on field weeks, based at Westward Ho! I returned with groups at least once a year for the whole of my career, first with school Geography pupils and then, when lecturing in Coastal Geomorphology at Oxford Brookes University, with specialist student groups.

My landscape and educational interests led me to design and write trails and landscape studies, first for the Field Studies Council, the Nature Conservancy Council and National Parks and then for the Geographical Association. In 1985, driven by a desire to expand the content of such studies to embrace a wider audience which would include the intellectually inquisitive, adult, non-specialist audience, and those seeking a greater understanding of the environment within which they live, my wife and I founded the educational publishing charity Thematic Trails. We eventually published some 14 booklets within North Devon (see page 128). In this book it has been my inclination to treat the coastal landscape as a broader canvas, if only because the commentary on each landscape photo is usually restricted to one page. Nevertheless, I recognised that readers might well wish to consult the more detailed information carried in the relevant Thematic Trail. My strategy has therefore been to flag the appropriate Thematic Trails by a coloured number (e.g. **7**). Other sources and quotes are flagged with a letter (e.g. C) so commentary pages may contain a small panel looking something like this: **1** **7** **A** **C**. The full titles can then be identified from 'Further reading' on page 126.

I would like to think that this book encourages people to explore some of the more remote parts of this glorious coast which might not be familiar to them. The two maps I found most useful are listed here. You may also like to have these maps by your side as you read. Like me, it might help you to further explore these cliffs in your imagination. Enjoy yourself. **Peter Keene 2nd October 2013**

Ordnance Survey *Explorer Maps* at a scale of 1:25,000
Map 126 Clovelly and Hartland (covers all the coast west of Westward Ho!).
Map 139 Bideford, Ilfracombe and Barnstaple (covers the coast east of Peppercombe).

Contents

4 Information for reader
HARTLAND ATLANTIC COAST
6 Higher Sharpnose Pt. Vicarage Cliff
8 Henna Cliff. Morwenstow
10 Cornakey Cliff
12 Litter Water. Devil's Hole
14 Marsland Mouth
16 Welcombe Mouth, Strawberry Water
18 Nabor Point. Embury Beacon
20 Milford Common. Green Ranger
24 Speke's Mill Mouth
30 St Catherine's Tor
32 Hartland Quay
40 Warren Cliff and Beach
42 Broad Beach
44 Blackpool Mill. Abbey River
46 Berry Cliff. Blegberry Beach
50 Damehole Point. Smoothlands
54 Hartland Point lighthouse. Johanna
BIDEFORD BAY
60 Chapman Rock
64 Beckland Water. Beckland Bay
68 Mouth Mill. Blackchurch Rock
72 Gallantry Bower. Gallant Cliff
74 Clovelly
78 Keivell's Wood
80 Bucks Mills
84 Worthygate Wood
86 Peppercombe, Portledge
88 Cockington. Tut's Hole
92 Green Cliff
94 Cornborough
98 Kipling Tors. Rock Nose. Seafield
104 Westward Ho!
114 Northam Burrows
118 Crow Point
122 Appledore
126 BIBLIOGRAPHY
127 ACKNOWLEDGEMENTS
128 THEMATIC TRAILS

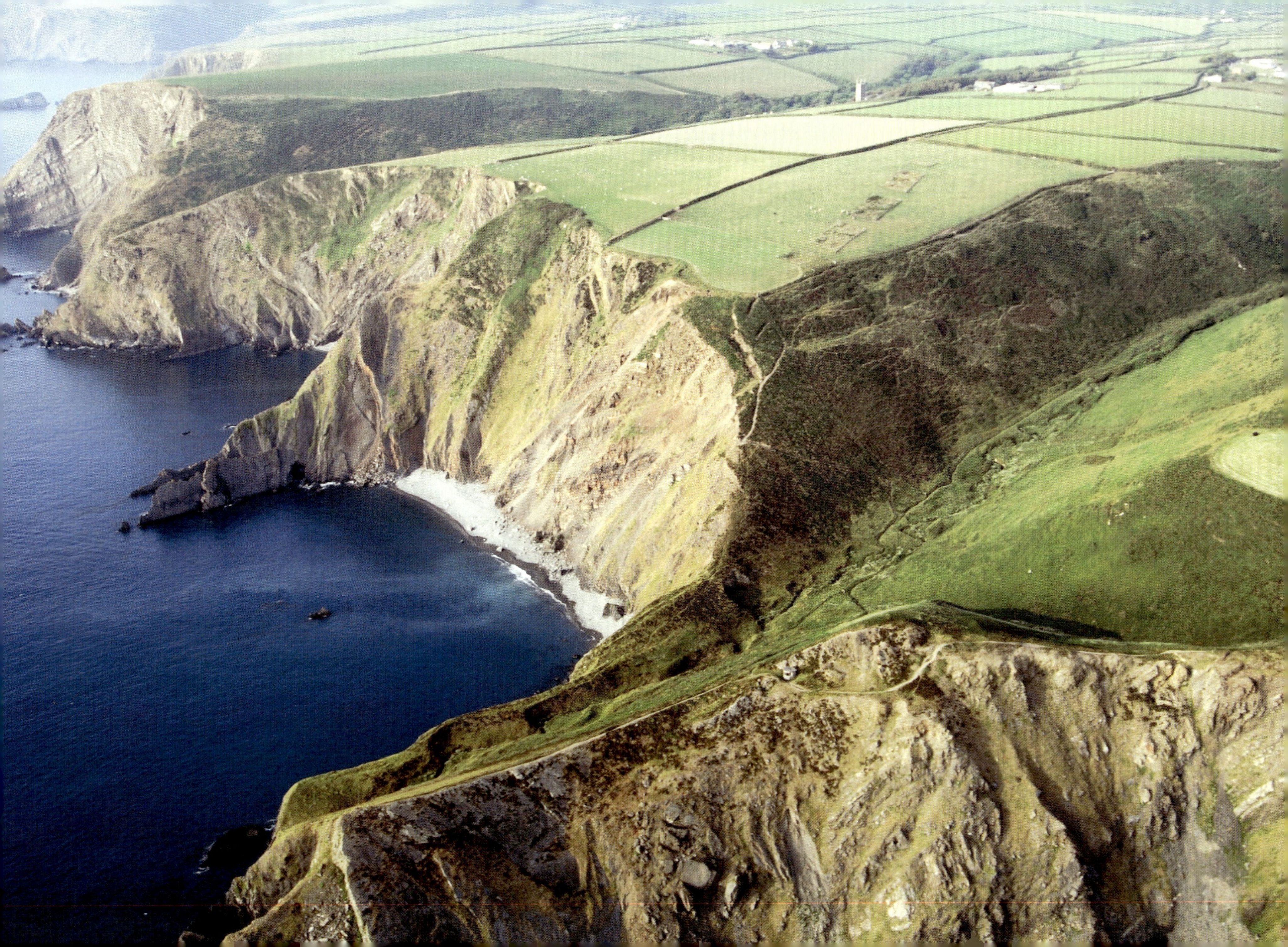

Higher Sharpnose looking north across the Tidna stream. Flying west over the green fields of the Plateau of North-West Devon the green fields suddenly drop away into the sea. This is the Atlantic Wall - cliffs which stretch nearly continuously from Hartland Point to Land's End - constantly being undermined at high tide by the crashing Atlantic surf - but not this evening (23 June 2009). In the distance Morwenstow Church peeps out from the sheltered flank of a small coombe. This is Hawker Country. Parson Hawker (1803-1875) came to this wild and remote Parish of Morwenstow in 1834. At the time there had been no vicar there for over 100 years. He proved an eccentric but compassionate vicar. A poet and writer, he soon built a driftwood shelter overlooking the sea where he would contemplate, so it is said, in the company of his opium pipe, and there study, write and watch the Atlantic shore. In a book of poems "*Reeds shaken with the wind*", published in 1844, he led with the following frontispiece:

THE FATHERS
They had their lodges in the wilderness,
Or built them cells beside the shadowy sea,
And there they dwelt with angels like a dream!
So they unclosed the volume of the book
And filled the fields of the evangelist,
With thoughts as sweet as flowers:
                                              Old Ms.

When he became more famous he entertained guests in his hut, including Alfred Tennyson and Charles Kingsley. Hawker's Hut still survives and is the smallest National Trust property.

The three fields seen beyond the stream called Tidna, are known as Vicarage Cliff. The hut, barely visible on the air photo, hangs on the cliff edge close to where the very long field boundary meets the cliff.

Higher Sharpnose northwards across Vicarage Cliff to Lucky Hole and beyond (Joe Keene circa 1960). Most of my father's art was triggered by landscape and he felt strongly that, before he painted, a landscape should be first experienced, absorbed and sketched, so much time was spend intimately exploring such areas of the North Devon coast.

"In the cloud shrouded cottage set beside flowing water one can forget the troubles of the world". (Chinese seal in the Ashmolean, Oxford)

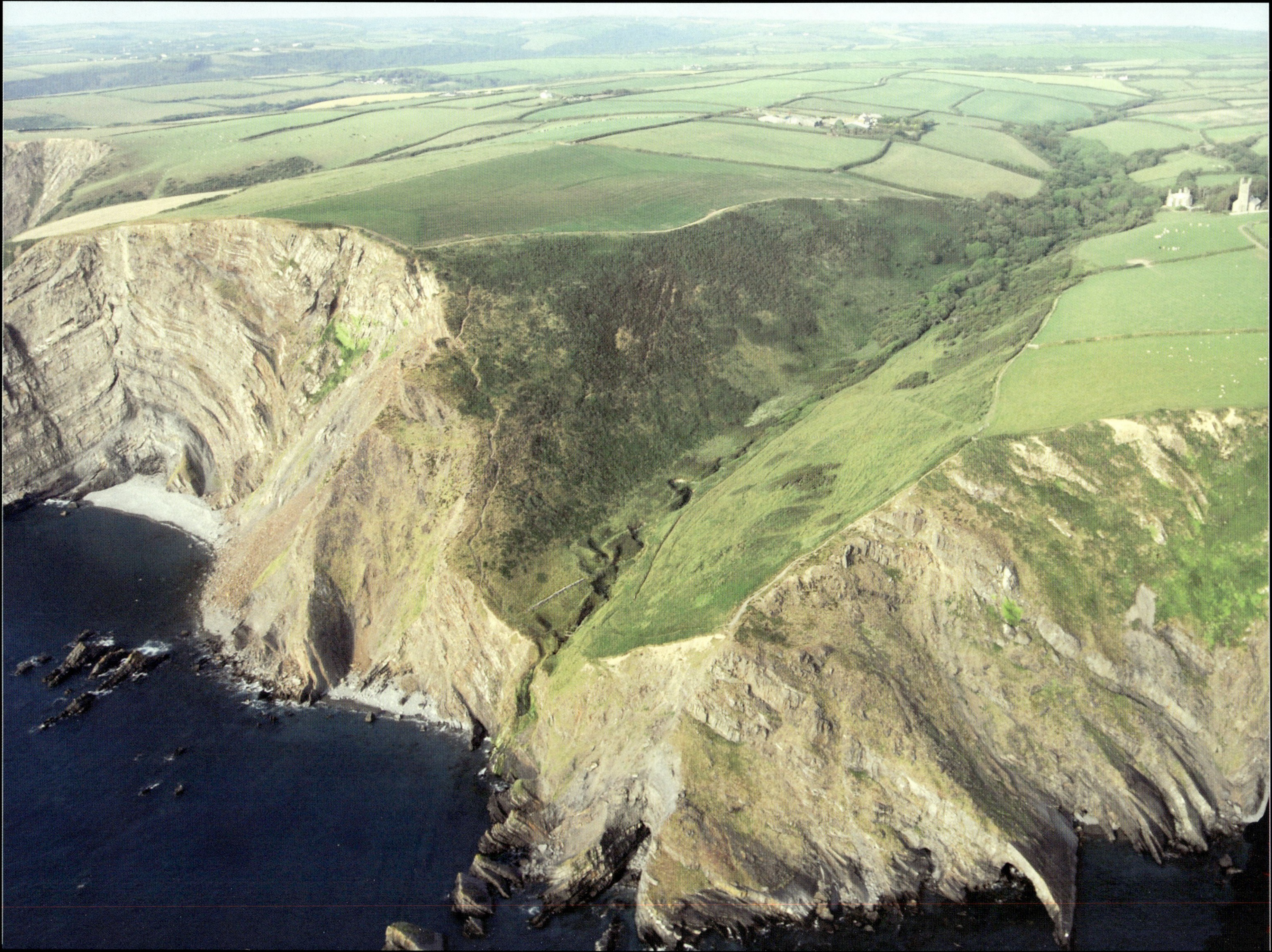

Henna Cliff (the Raven's crag). The coastal plateau is notched by coombs, themselves truncated by eroding cliffs. Morwenstow church and Vicarage is on the right-hand edge of the air photo. The remarkable vicarage was designed by Hawker himself who had the following inscription carved in stone in the porch of his vicarage:

> "A House, a Glebe, a Pound a day;*
> A Pleasant Place to Watch and Pray,
> Be true to Church; Be kind to the poor,
> O Minister for evermore."
>
> * When Hawker arrived the living was worth £365 p.a.

The parish church is dedicated to Saints John the Baptist and Morwenna. Over time, the Reverend Hawker buried in his churchyard some forty sailors who had the misfortune to be wrecked, drowned and washed ashore beneath Hawker's Hut. One such wreck (1842) was the 'Caledonia' a brig of some 200 tons with a crew of nine, from Arbroath, Scotland. All bar one were drowned. A memorial erected in the churchyard to mark the graves of the captain and crew, was a white figurehead rescued from the wreck. In 2006, having suffered from the ravages of time, the figurehead was removed for conservation, being replaced by a replica. The original is now displayed inside the church.

> "We laid them in their lowly rest,
> The strangers of a distant shore;
> We smoothed the green turf on their breast,
> 'Mid baffled Ocean's angry roar;
> And there, the relique of the storm,
> We fixed fair Scotland's figured form.
>
> She watches by her bold, her brave,
> Her shield towards the fatal sea:
> Their cherished lady of the wave
> Is guardian of their memory.
> Stern is her look, but calm, for there
> No gale can rend or billow bear."

The Hartland coast suffered many wrecks in the days of sail, as saw-toothed reefs, cast seawards from the shore entrapped coastal vessels on this lee shore. In 1859 after a particularly fierce storm caused several wrecks, Hawker wrote:

B

> "Full 50 years it is said since we had such a storm. Limbs are cast ashore every now and then, arms and legs, and at Hartland joining Welcombe, lumps of flesh have floated above High water, and been buried in the ground. Five out of Seven Corpses had no Heads – cut off by the jagged rocks!! Since 1843 I have taken up from the rocks and buried 27. But to me the great comfort is, that the souls of all these men are grateful to me for the respectful interment of their bodies, and that all they are permitted to do for me they fulfil. That they have brought me tokens of goodwill I am persuaded."

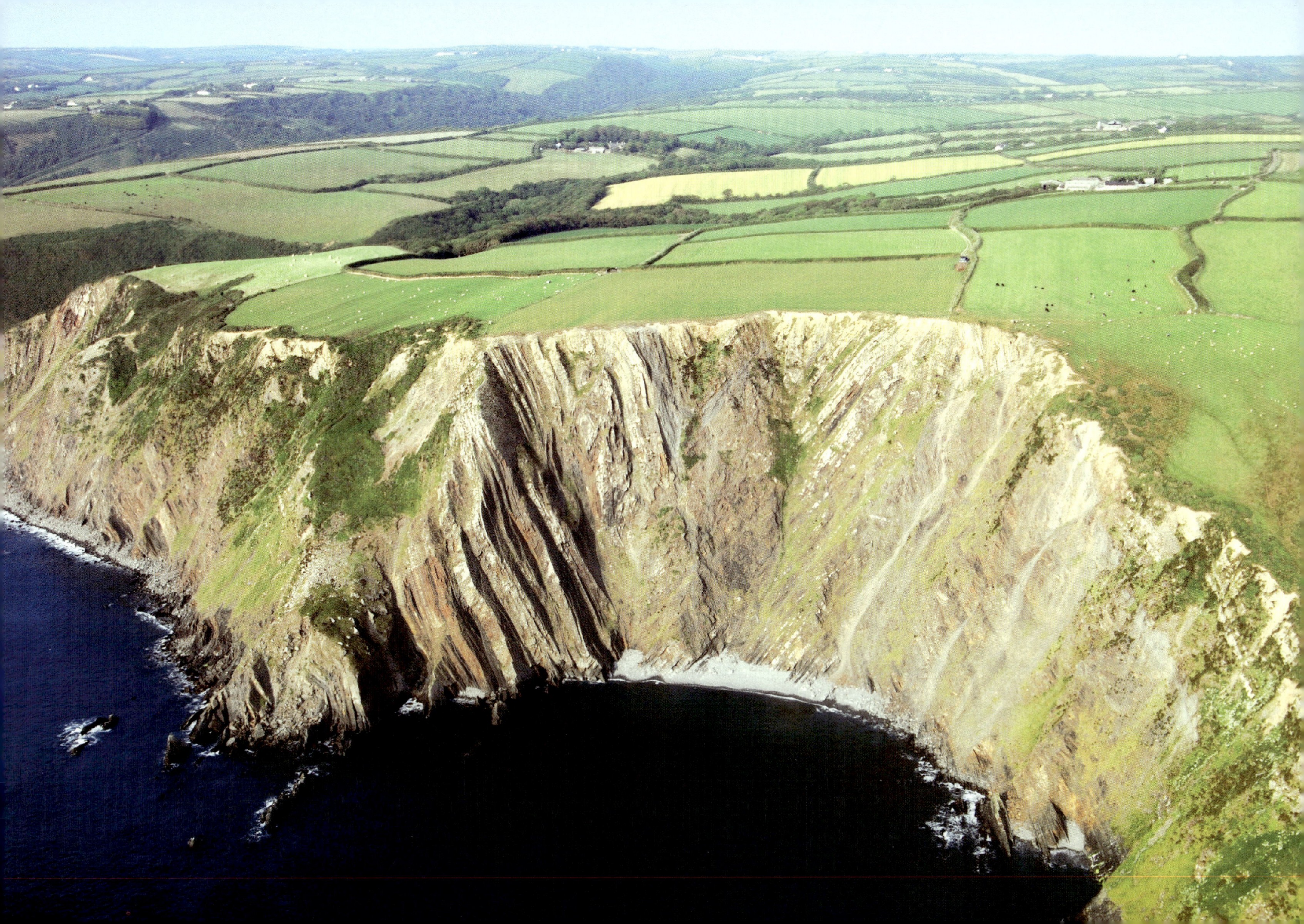

On this Atlantic-facing coast, steeply folded rock beds strike out to sea.

Cornakey Cliff

As you may see on the left hand side of the air photo of Cornakey Cliff, the harder more resistant beds of rock stand proud of the cliff. In many places along this Atlantic coast, these tough sandstone beds strike or run out seawards forming reefs which have always been a particular threat to ships that ply this coast. An even greater danger in the days of sail was that this was a lee shore, that is, the winds most commonly blew from the sea towards the shore, so that sailing vessels commonly had cliffs on their lee side, the side to which they were naturally driven by the wind. As the Admiralty caution suggests - not good news.

ADMIRALTY CAUTION FOR SAILING VESSELS (West Coast of England 1902)

'In the approach to the Bristol Channel, there is always a ground swell setting in from about W.N.W., unless easterly winds have long prevailed . . . Its effect is to impel a vessel towards the Cornish...or Devonshire coast. It is worthy of remark that with the wind westward of South there is scarcely a safe roadstead for a sailing vessel between Land's End and Flatholm island in the Bristol Channel, with the exception of Lundy and Clovelly roads . . . Should a sailing vessel (become embayed), the crew should stick to their ship, as, with the many life-saving appliances established along the coast, there is every chance of being saved. There is little or no chance of saving life by taking to the ship's boats, owing to the heavy and confused sea, which at times renders even life-boats unmanageable.'

Reefs running seawards, seen from Higher Sharpnose looking north.

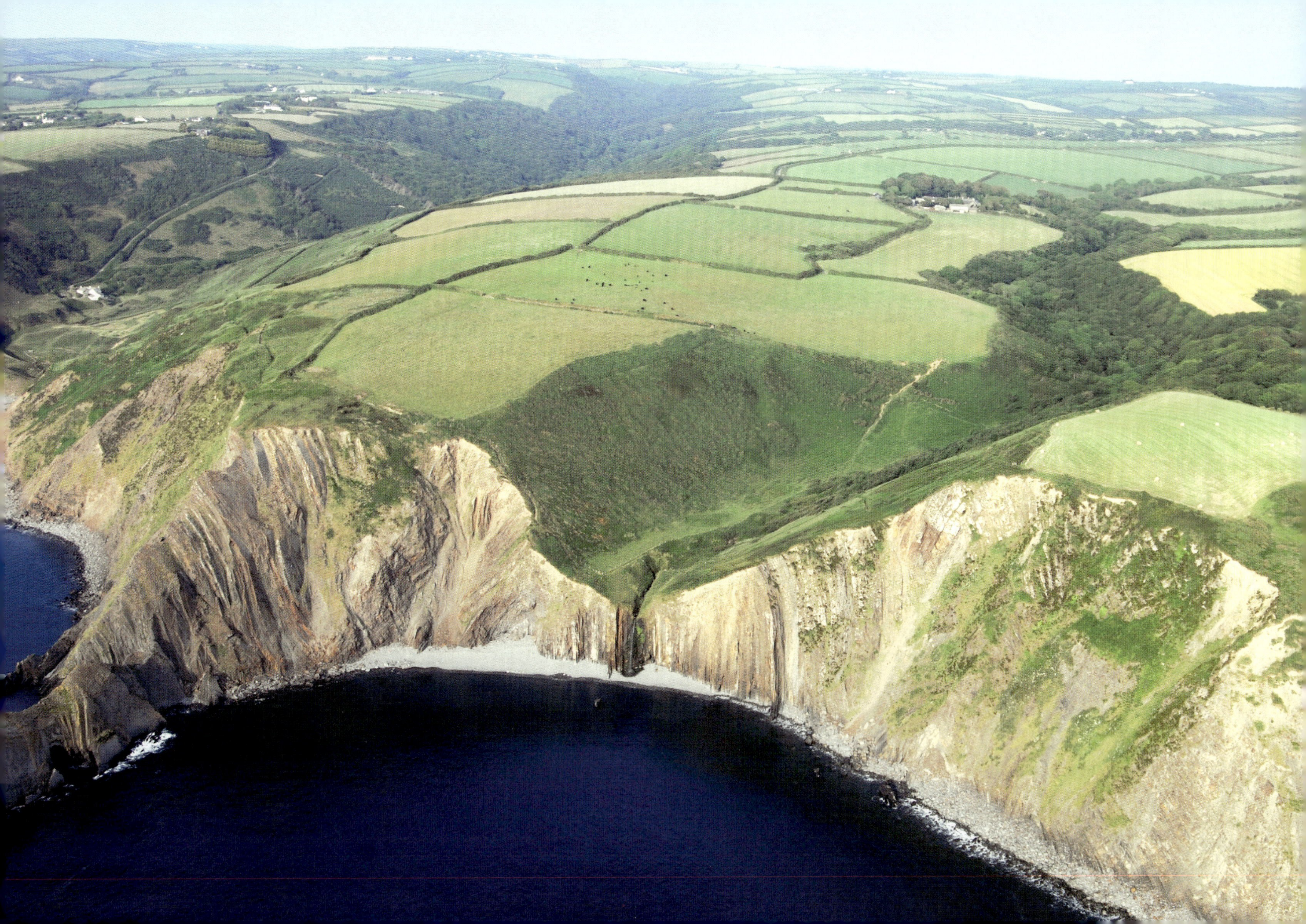

Litter Water   A short steep-sided coombe, truncated by sea erosion creating a coastal waterfall. The sides of these north coast coombes are too steep for cultivation and towards the sea the salt-laden on-shore winds preclude the growth of woodland although away from the sea the valley sides become clothed in trees which trace the valley form inland. In the hazy distance, about three miles away, is the watershed which separates these short north-draining streams from the south-flowing tributaries of the Tamar which flows into Plymouth Sound. Close by, on the same watershed, tributaries of the Torridge loop inland before eventually draining north again into Bideford Bay.

To the left of Litter Mouth is Gull Rock, a stack at high tide, which brings to mind the new freedom of exploration which I acquired when I took to sea kayaking seriously. In April 1972 I retired my self-built canvas and lath Percy Blanchard Kayak, a kayak which I always took to the sea in North Devon with extreme caution, and bought a new fibreglass Klepper 'Munchen', (£44). This coast has its dangers but the attraction for me was not so much the agreeable physical expenditure of learning how to punch successfully against wind, waves and tide, but the access a kayak can provide to explore hidden inaccessible coves, caves, galleries of birds and tiny sandy beaches. 'Munchen' provided all that. Log: 9th August 1976: *"Spent the day with a friend, kayaking gently from Duck Pool to Hartland Quay. Gull Rock is punctured by a tall sea-cave called the Devil's Hole. If the breakers are small and the tide is right it is quite simple to negotiate."* Paddling through from north to south for the first time, in reality from Devon to Cornwall, it is a thrill when suddenly you emerge to be greeted unexpectedly by a great panorama of Cornish cliffs.

| 1 | 2 |

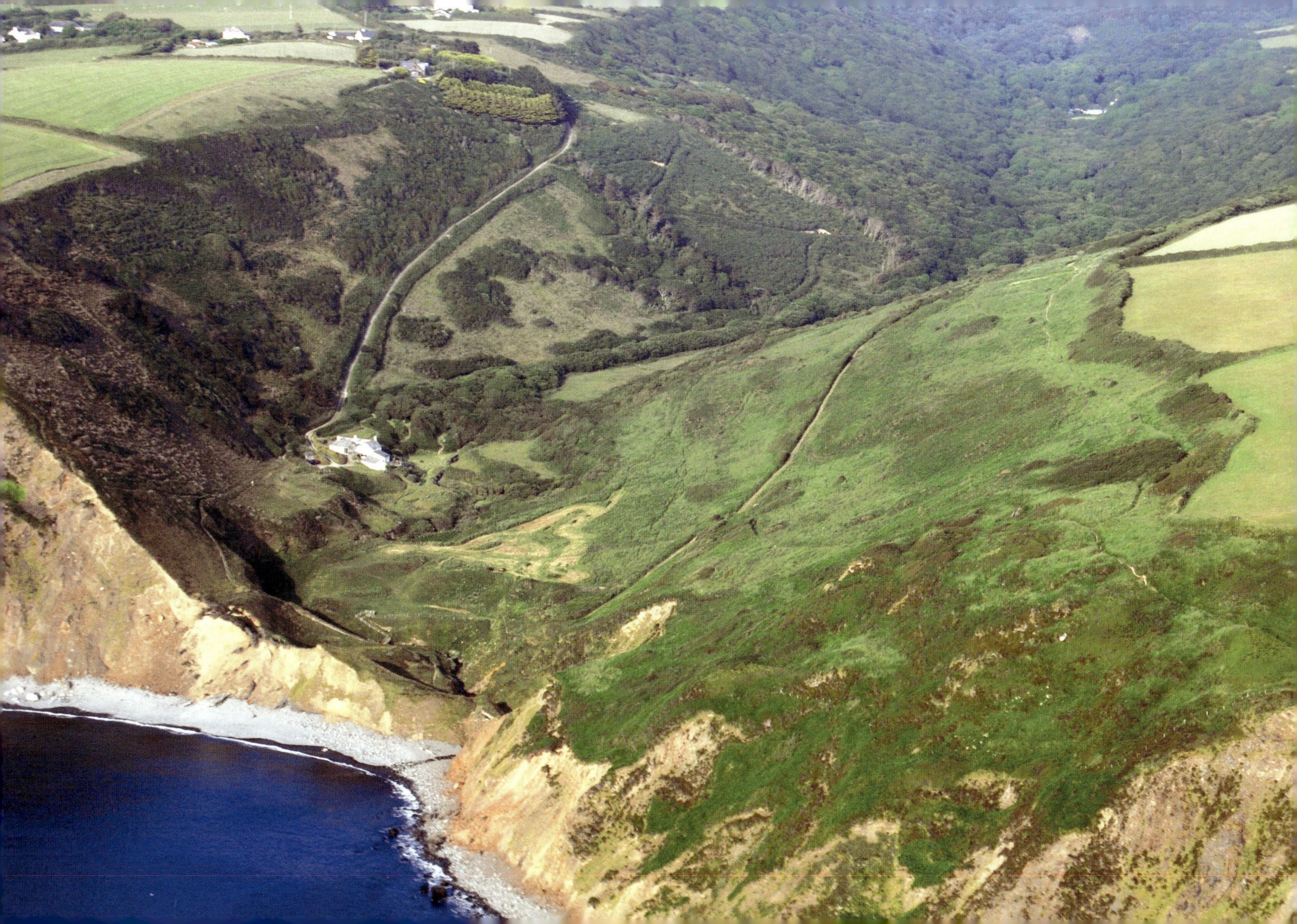

Marsland Mouth

C 1 2

"....those delightful glens, which cut the high table-land of the confines of Devon and Cornwall, and opening each through its gorge of down and rock, towards the boundless western ocean. Each is like the other, and each is like no other English scenery. Each has its upright walls, inland of rich oak-wood, nearer the sea of dark green furze, then of smooth turf, then of weird, black cliffs which range out right and left far into the deep sea, in castles, spires, and wings of jagged iron-stone. Each has its narrow strip of fertile meadow, it crystal trout-stream, winding across and across from one hill-foot to the other; its gray stone mill, with the water sparkling and humming round the dripping wheel; its dark rock pools above the tide mark, where the salmon-trout gather in from their Atlantic wanderings, after each autumn flood; its ridge of blown sand, bright with golden trefoil and crimson lady's finger; its gray bank of polished pebbles, down which the stream rattles toward the sea below. Each has its black field of jagged shark's-tooth rock which paves the cove from side to side, streaked with here and there a pink line of shell-sand, and laced with white foam from the eternal surge, stretching in parallel lines out to the westward, in strata set upright on edge, or tilted towards each other at strange angles by primeval earthquakes - such is the 'mouth' and that mouth as those coves are called; and such the jaw of teeth which they display, one rasp of which would grind abroad the timbers of the stoutest ship. To landward, all richness, softness, and peace; to seaward, a waste and howling wilderness of rock and roller, barren to the fisherman, and hopeless to the shipwrecked mariner.

In only one of these 'mouths' is a landing for boats, made possible by a long sea-wall of rock, which protects it from the rollers of the Atlantic;and that mouth is Marsland, the abode of the White Witch, Lucy Passmore;"

Thus opens 'The Coombes of the Far West', a chapter in Charles Kingsley's 'Westward Ho!' (1855). It is a prelude to a dramatic confrontation on the beach involving the Rose of the Torridge, Rose Salterne of Bideford.

Marsland Mouth coombe with West Mill and terraces.

By means of a weir built some 500 metres upstream, water was directed by a leat along the valley side to West Mill. This once created enough 'head' of water to drive a waterwheel as the water fell back into the stream. The route of the old abandoned leat can still be traced along the valley side.

Marsland Mouth is an SSSI, notably for its wildlife and ecological interest. It also has some interesting landforms. Under former cold-climate conditions the valley was in-filled with valley-side slope debris, finer pale material crowded with angular rock fragments. Remnants of this pale 'head' can still be seen in the cliff which marks the seaward end of the valley and also in the gently sloping surface between the Mill and the hillside. Subsequently, under warmer conditions the stream reasserted itself, cutting back down into this debris, carving a sequence of flat terraces and abandoned meanders marking stages in its progress.

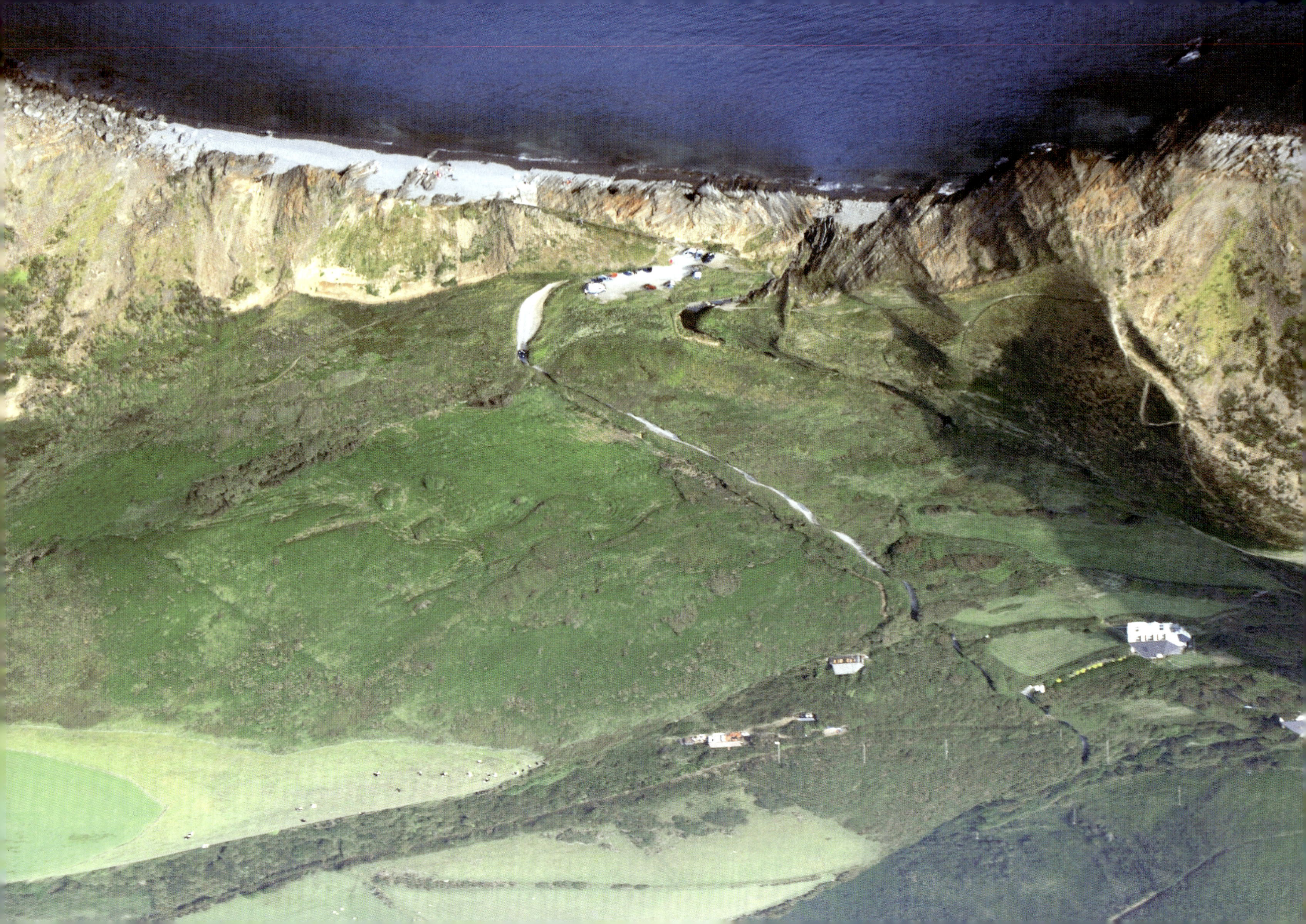

Welcombe Mouth

The Strawberry Water overcomes its last rock impediment before cascading down onto the beach.

The making of a pebble: Look at the cliff above. Beds of less resistant dark grey mudstones and harder, pale grey sandstone alternate across the cliff. The beds of sandstone often have an orange tinge due to superficial iron staining along joints but where these sandstone beds touch the beach, sand and stones agitated by waves (abrasion), have already polished the stone until its 'natural' light grey is exposed. These beds proceed seawards - look (bottom left) at pebble forms emerging. That is not the end of the story. Once formed, pebbles and shingle rubbing together in the surf (attrition) suffer mutual wear and tear until all is eventually reduced to sand.

Attrition is something you can hear. Visit Welcombe Mouth at high tide, sit on the beach, close your eyes and listen.

Listen! you hear the grating roar
Of pebbles which the waves draw back, and fling,
At their return, up the high strand,
Begin, and cease, and then again begin,
With tremulous cadence slow, and bring
The eternal note of sadness in.

            Matthew Arnold (Dover Beach).

Beach exposed at low tide

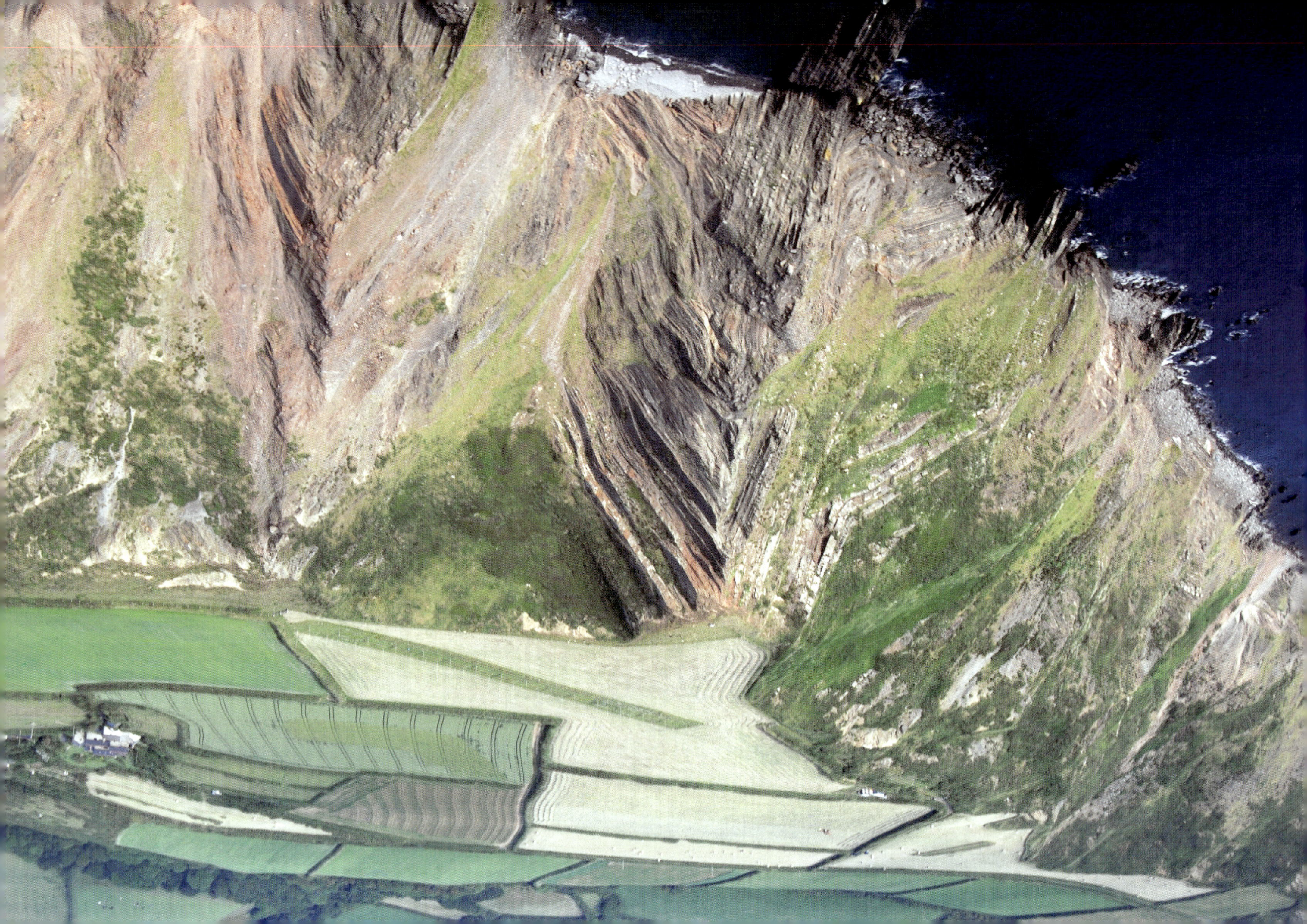

Nabor Point. Impressive steep upright folds. The hamlet 400 metres inland is South Hole. *South (off right) is Embury Beacon hillfort and Broadbench Cove. Off left is Sandhole Cliff. From here road-side cliff views are spectacular both south and north (spot the wreck).* A 3

Walking the cliff-top path in the early 1970s my interest was caught by a small remnant of an Iron Age (200BC) hill fort at Embury Beacon. It was clear it must once have been much more extensive. With an academic interest in coastal evolution and cliff retreat, I contacted the helicopter base at Chivenor and asked if, in passing, someone might like to take a black and white air photo for me (see right). On reflection, I concluded that as there was no way of accurately judging the former extent of this promontory hillfort, I could not realistically suggest a rate of cliff retreat and so I let the matter rest.

However, excavations in 1972-3 and rescue digs in 2012 regenerated interest. A site map (mid-right) showed some erosion since my photo and furthermore marked a proposed area (in red) for a possible former extent of the hill fort. If this is an accurate reconstruction it would enable a rough guide to the minimum rate of cliff erosion per year (i.e. distance from the tip of the present headland to the outermost corner of the red line marking the projected extent of the hillfort divided by 2213).

Beneath Embury Beacon is Broadbench Cove a spectacular site (lower right) I 'discovered' when I began exploring this shore in detail using my new Munchen kayak (bottom right). I, of course, was not the first. Geologist Newell Arber (The Coastal Scenery of North Devon) writing in 1911 of this site commented:

"... the finest examples of contorted rocks to be found for many miles up or down this coast. Several faults are seen in the cliff, and thus the folds, which consist of alternate layers of sandstones and shales of nearly equal thickness, are thrown into indescribable confusion."

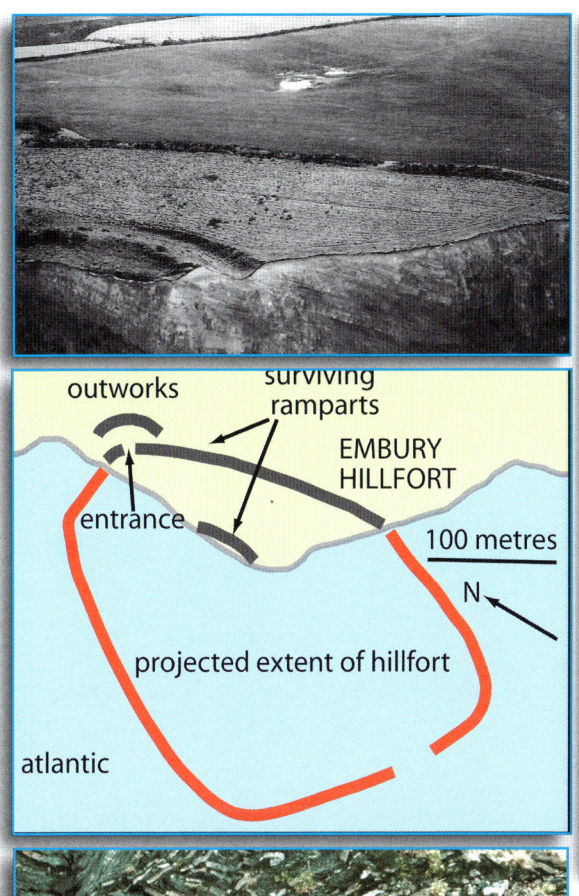

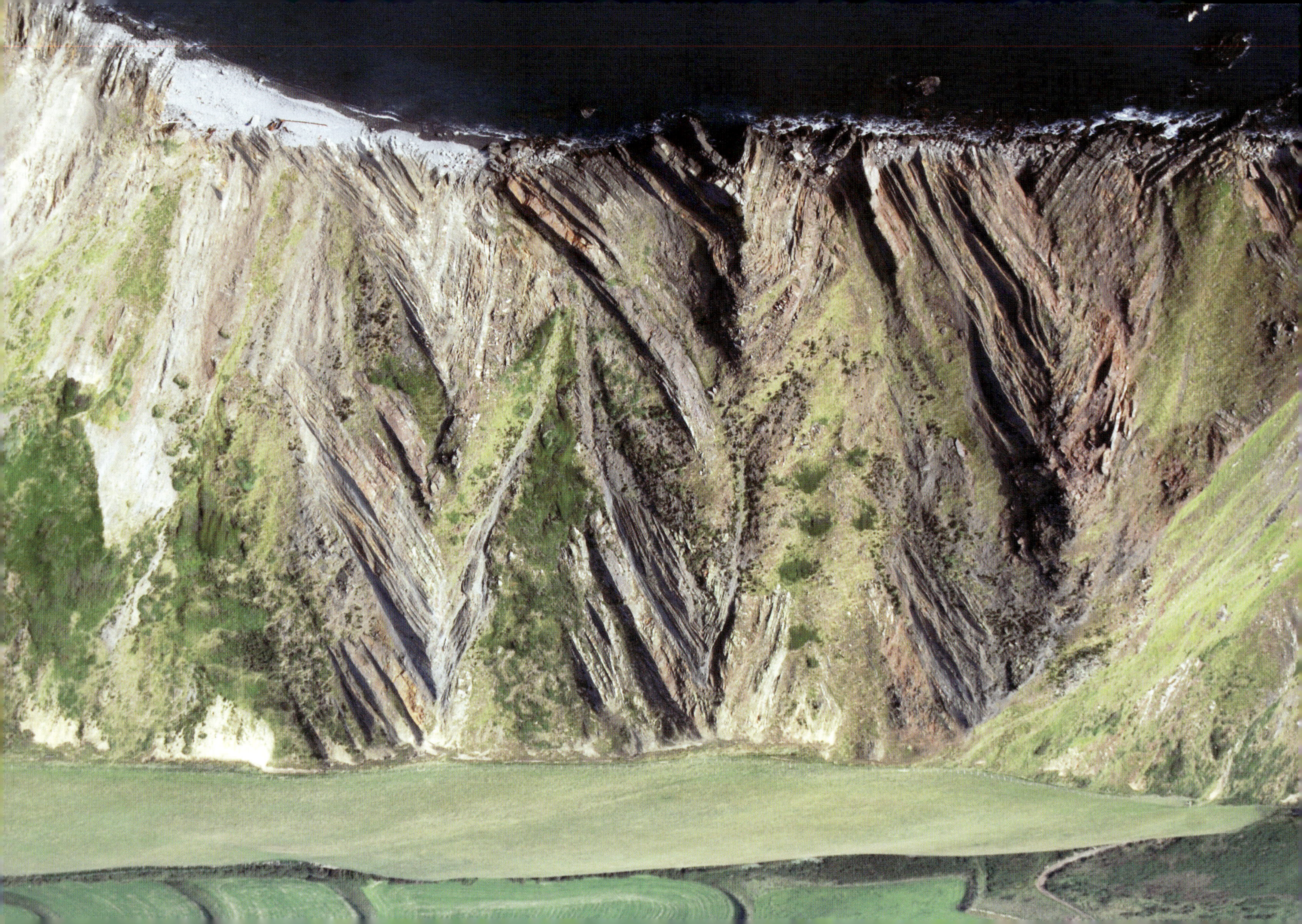

Milford Common. This overlooks Longpeak Beach and Gunpath Rock. Walking along the coastal path on Milford Common there is no immediate clue of what lies just beneath your feet. Yet think of the intense forces necessary to fold these once near-horizontal sea-floor beds of sediments into the vertical folds, the violent memory of which can be seen in these 110 metre (360 foot) sea cliffs hereabouts.

Local reefs continued to claim ships long after the days of sail. On 17th November 1962, the **Green Ranger**, a 3000-ton Royal Fleet Auxiliary tanker, was being towed to South Wales for refit when, in heavy seas, the cables parted and the vessel, adrift, was swept onto Gunpath Reef. The wreck can be seen in the 1963 photo of the coast from Sandhole Cliff on page 19.

The skeleton crew of seven 'stuck to their ship' and were rescued by breeches buoy. Within the month the vessel broke in two and any idea of refloating was abandoned. More valuable metallic objects were winched to the cliff top. Relics are displayed in Hartland Quay Museum. The portholes grace the Wrecker's Bar (for a time known as the Green Ranger bar).

3 1 4

Wrecks fascinate. I visited The Green Ranger many times. Initially walking across the rocks from Speke's Mill Mouth. I remember in 1963 how I sat mesmerised, listening to the metallic hollow booming of waves entering the ship. Somewhere a door or hatch slammed as it must have done at every high tide since November 1962.

The acorn barnacle encrusted engine room of the Green Ranger in 1974, twelve years after the wreck struck Gunpath Rock

Green Ranger revisited Kayaking alone along the coast, the Green Ranger became a regular call, although often I could not land. On rare occasions I tempted the odd friend to join me, hence the kayak photos. By 1974 the main body of the ship, the great steel plates, had been pushed relentlessly towards the cliff foot, leaving behind, virtually in situ, the heavy engine room, and the boilers, which usually outlast the main body of a wreck by many years.

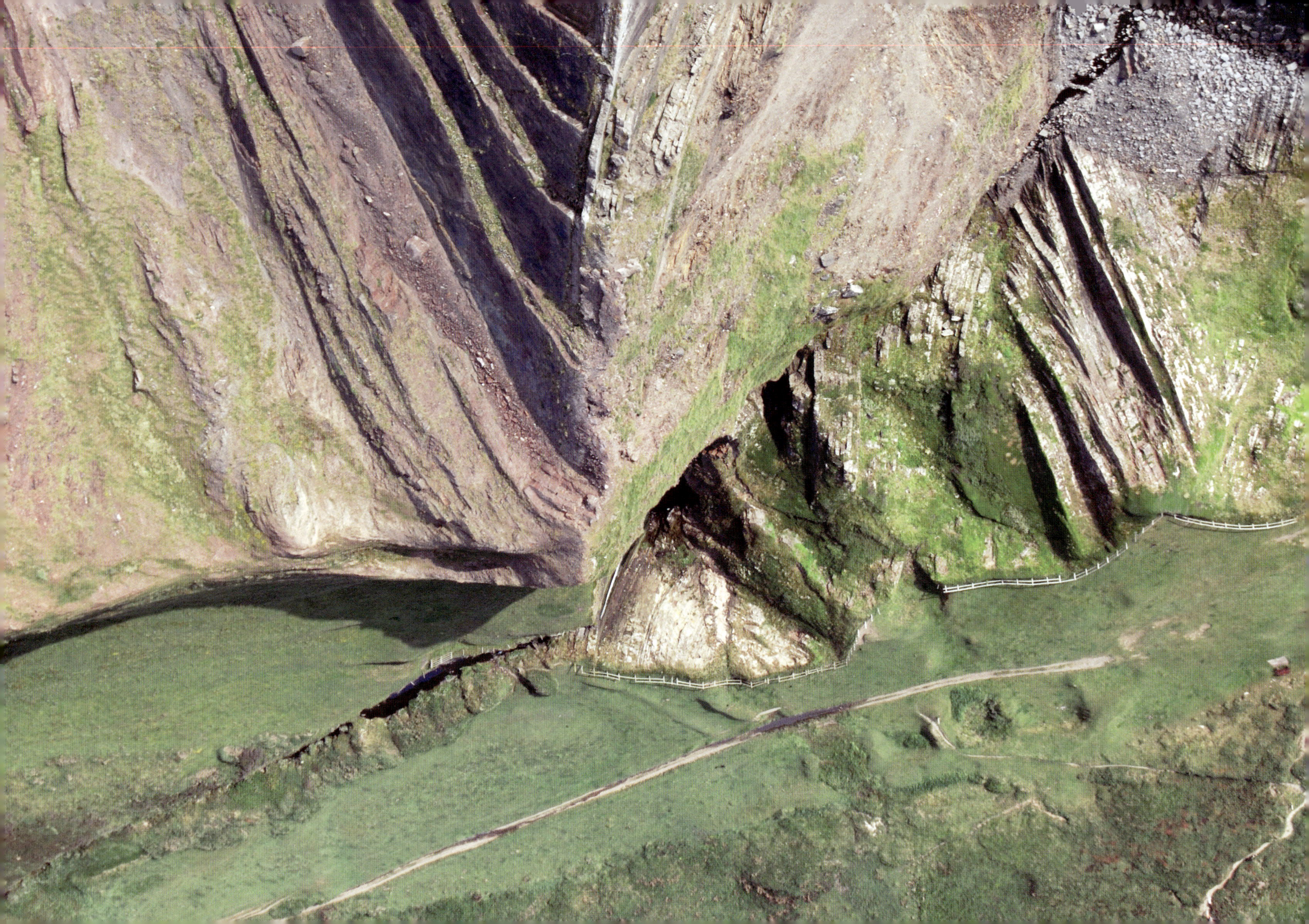

"Undoubtedly, when the existence of this fall becomes better known, it will be an object of pilgrimage." E A Newell Arber, 1911

Speke's Mill Mouth - a hidden waterfall. This is the 'mouth' of the Milford Water, which is suddenly truncated by the sea whilst still 48 metres (157 feet) above sea level, creating a spectacular chain of waterfalls. One reason for this fall being so impressive is that it is hidden from you until the last moment. Walking out from Hartland Quay you will make a steep descent into the Milford Water valley where you might pause, but then, perhaps attracted by the background noise of falling water, you walk across the grass towards the sound but it isn't until you reach the fence that the view of the upper fall suddenly opens out beneath you.

Summer flow

Winter freeze

Autumn spate is achieved rapidly after a few hours of heavy rainfall on saturated ground.

3 1 A

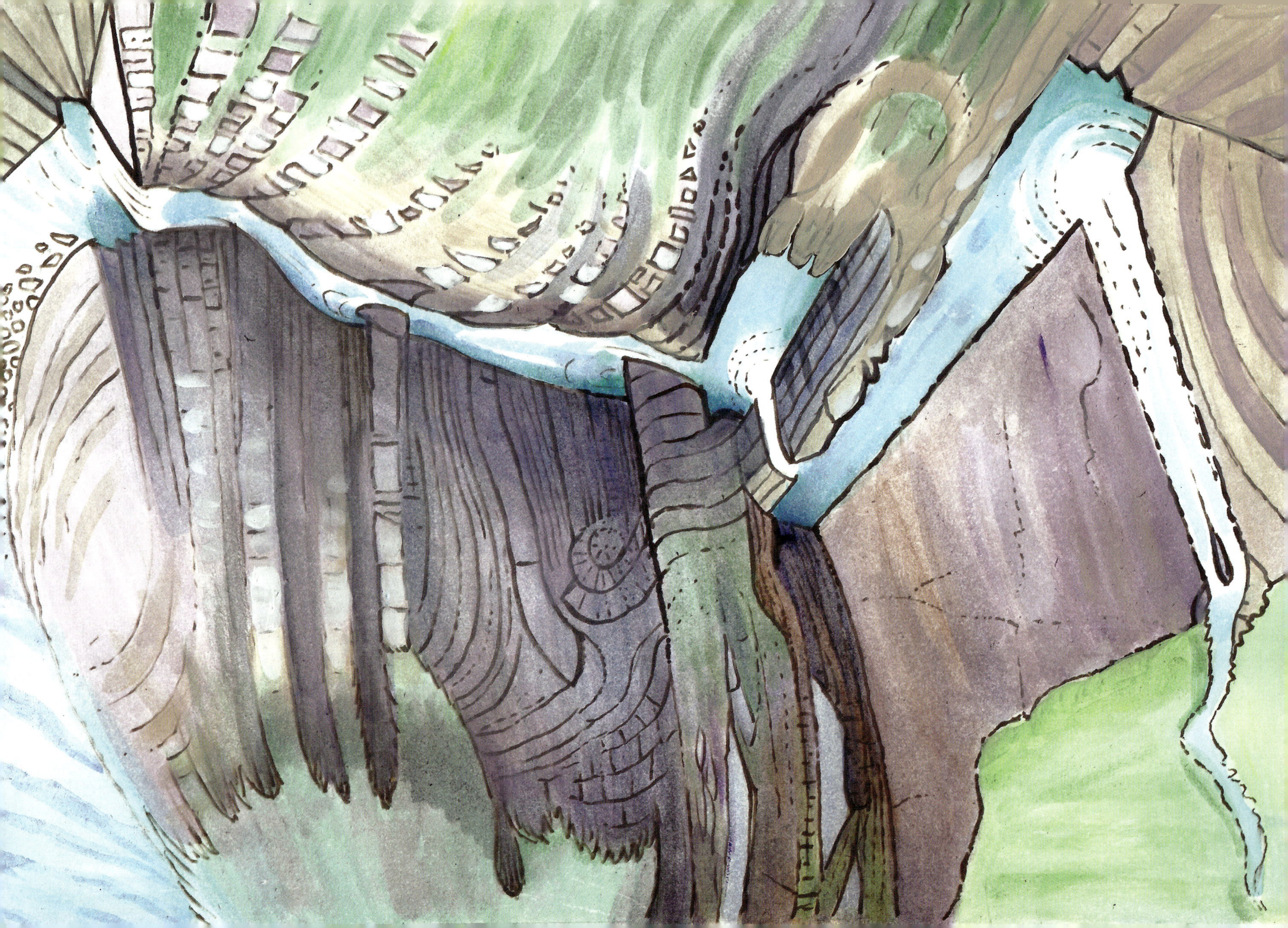

Speke's Mill Mouth

Left: Air photo taken on 23rd June 2009.

Flying over Speke's Mill Mouth, I marvelled at the complexity of the geology and the way, both vertically and horizontally, the stream course was being directed by the angle of the various beds of rock. Knowing his work as a landscape artist, I commissioned Kester Webb to produce a work to demonstrate his take on this intriguing and complex mixture of the passage of water and the intense rock folding – to do this for Speke's Mill Mouth, I thought would be no mean task. Well, he has produced something in his inimitable style, (unique and impossible to imitate). It is an investigation of the place which adds a level of description which no photograph can hope to emulate (see drawing above).

> Kester Webb. September 2013:
> *"My drawing is an artist's impression created from a series of photographs and sketches focussing on the rock formations inside the canyon. My style of drawing emphasises the complex tilting and folding of the bedding planes."*

Figures above the first fall at Speke's Mill Mouth

3 1 A F

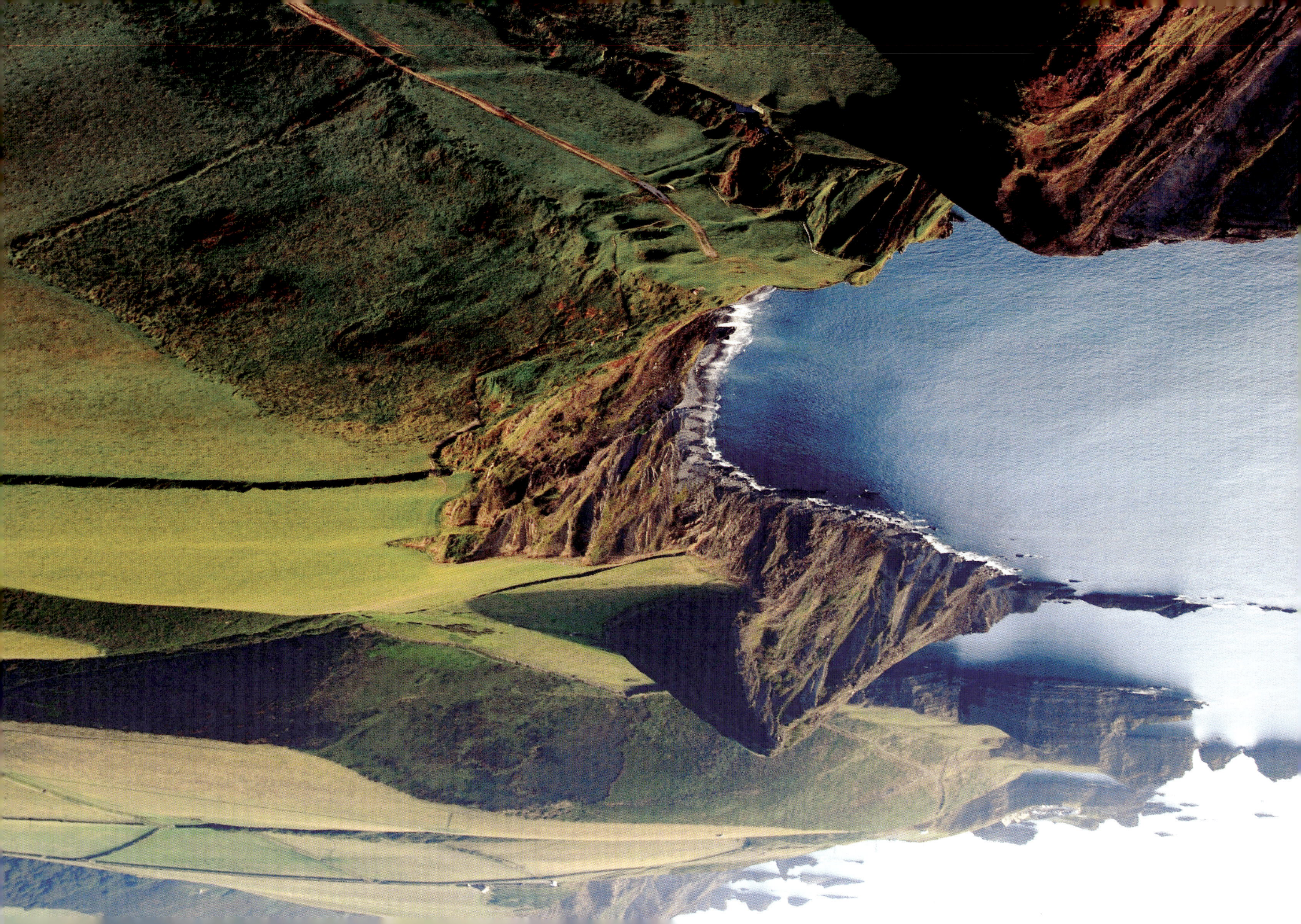

Above: **Speke's Mill Mouth** looking north towards Hartland Quay

Right: A page from Inkermann Roger's notebook (1907). "There are four waterfalls at Speke's Mill Mouth, the top fall is the highest and greatest. It is 53 feet 9 inches."

The Hartland Peninsula. *"It contains the most impressive cliff scenery in England and Wales, above all the iron coast from Hartland Point southwards, with its coastal waterfalls. The seascapes are superb, for there is no land between this coast and America."*

W.G. Hoskins 1954.

The Milford Water disappears over the cliff edge descending to the beach in a series of falls controlled by the local geology. A footpath also disappears over the cliff in a zig-zag descent to the beach. The path was originally used to enable pack-donkeys to ferry sand from the beach to the sand lews (open storage pens) on the valley floor at the top of the cliff path. There it would be stored before distribution to local farmsteads to be put on the land. The remains of the lews can still be seen today on the valley floor near the top of the first waterfall. To read more about the route by which the Milford Water originally made its way to the sea, read 'The Cliffs of Hartland Quay' (**3**).

One of the characteristics of much of this coast are the flat-topped cliffs, punctured at intervals by the short but steep-sided coastal coombes. The flat surface of Milford Common is particularly impressive and gives a mile or so of welcome relief to coastal walkers who are more accustomed to negotiating the frequent deep coombes which dissect this plateau edge.

The photo (left) was taken on a very calm day. No zephyr cooled my cheek and yet a long slow swell pulsed in, perhaps from Labrador?

*"Where on Hartland's tempest-furrowed shore
Breaks the long swell from farthest Labrador."*

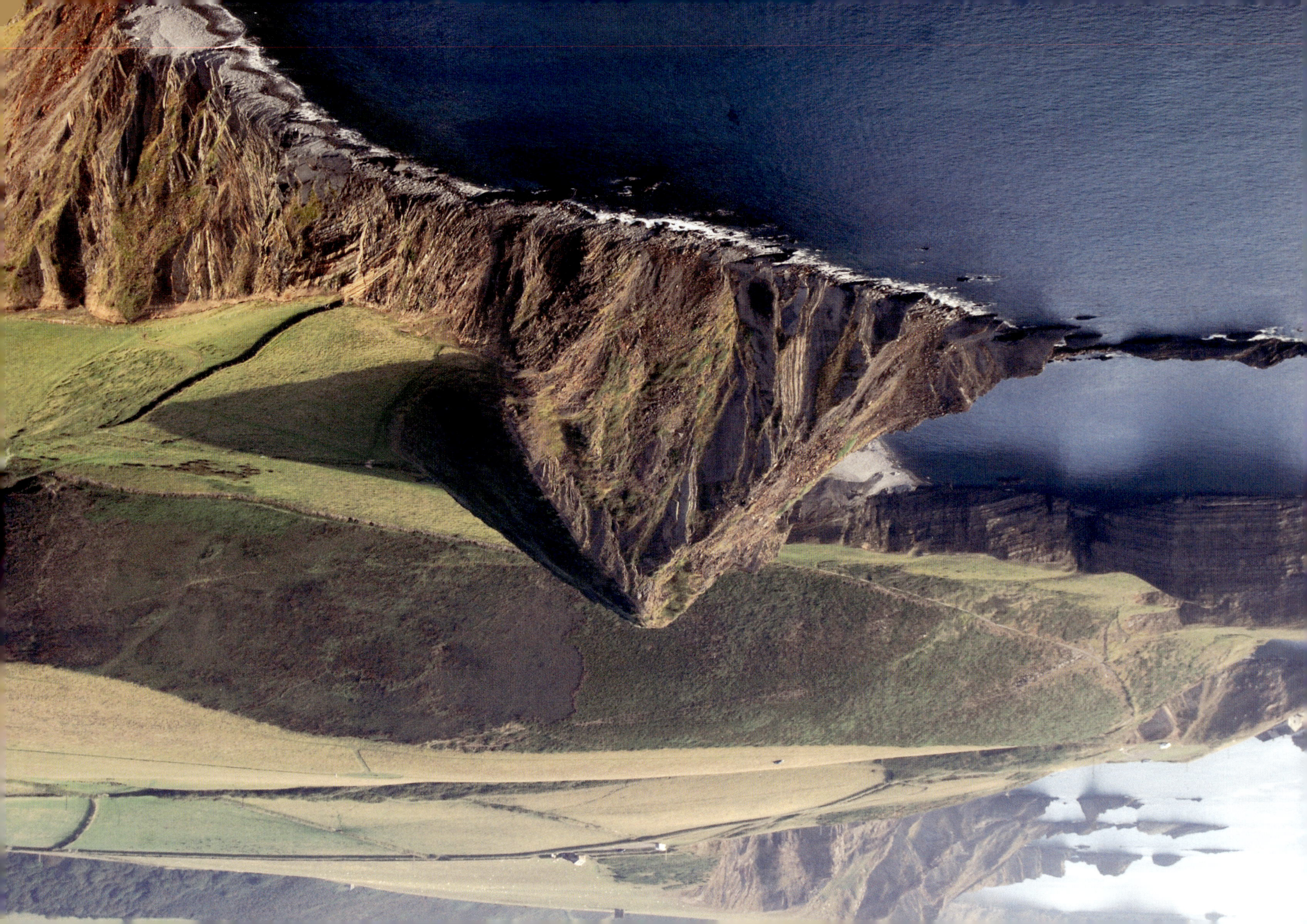

St Catherine's Tor The summit was always a stop on my cliff top walks with students on annual field trips. We would sit in a convenient flat, grassy platform, a land slip surface, just one step down from the seaward side of the summit. However, after 20 years or so of such visits, it was an active scramble down the cliff face to this grassy platform which now sloped landwards. From the aircraft (23 June 2009) I looked in vain for this little picnic spot. The landward side of St Catherine's Tor is clothed in thick vegetation and it takes some effort to climb to the peak but the view from the top is worth it. However, do not attempt it in a strong wind. It is reported that a medieval chapel once crowned the tor-top but if so it has long ago slipped into the sea. The seaward side of the hill has the scarred appearance of a slope being actively eroded by the sea.

From St Catherine's Tor looking south to beyond Speke's Mouth beach

Commissioned in 2005 to paint a cover for *The Cliffs of Hartland Quay*, Paul Lewin, as is his custom, hauled his equipment and canvas (72 x 55 cm) up to the summit to work in the field on the main structure of his painting.

In strong winds we nearly lost Paul and his painting. The multimedia finished product (left) was completed later in his studio.

Looking up a photo I had taken some years earlier (right) I wondered what exactly, for me, made the painting resonate so much more strongly of a sense of place than my photograph.

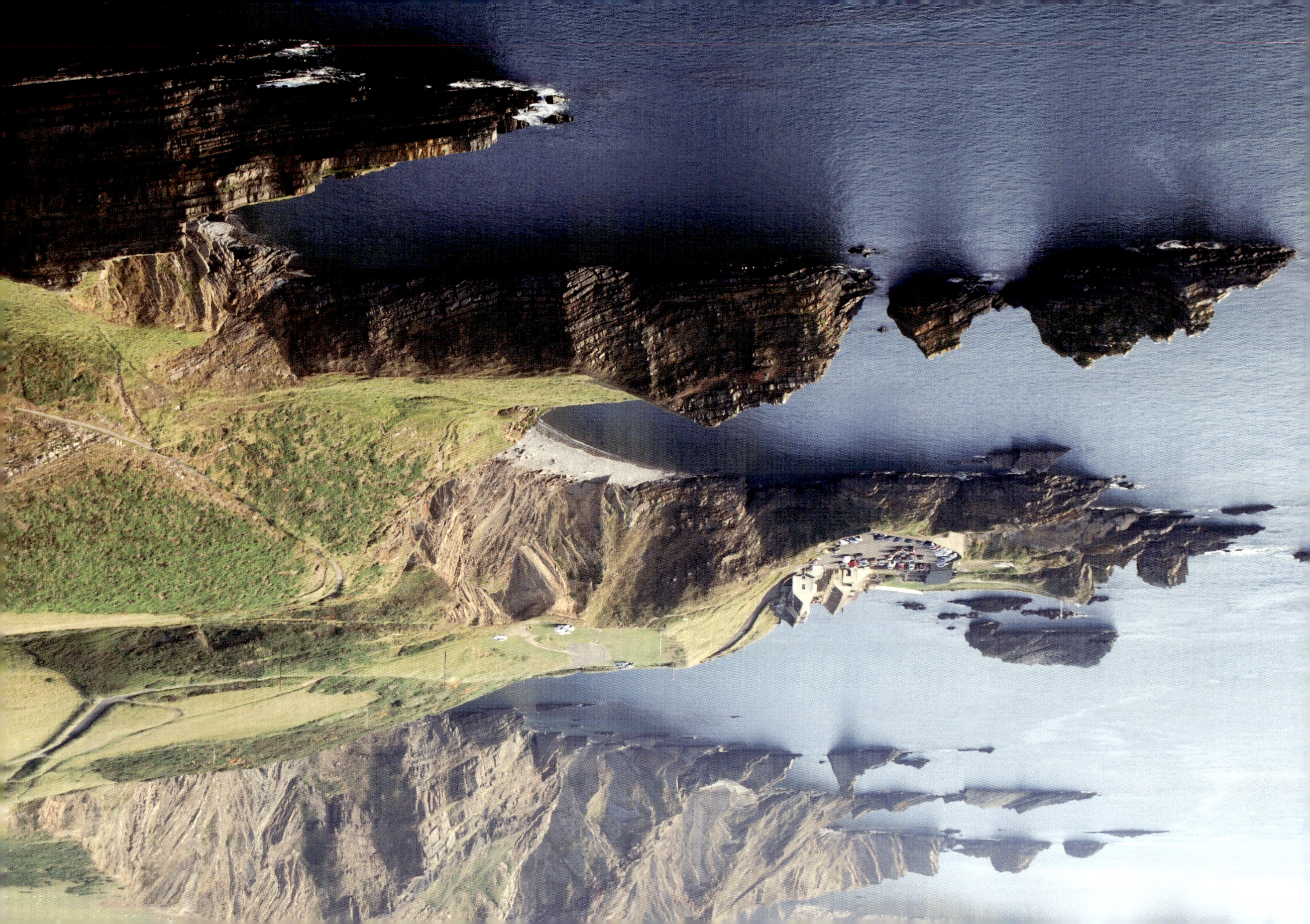

Screda Point, Well Beach and Hartland Quay Hotel

"Hartland Quay is usually reached by driving (three hours) from Bideford, which is on the L. & S. W. Railway from London, Exeter, and Barnstaple to Torrington. There is also a Post-office mail brake twice a day from Bideford, via Clovelly Cross, to Hartland Town, where one can arrange to be met by a trap from the Hartland Quay hotel. This is a cheap and rapid means of reaching Hartland, provided one is only encumbered with a small amount of luggage. There are also carriers' carts to Hartland Town on certain days of the week, which may be patronized but they are very slow."

A.E. Newell Arber (1911)

Right, the coastal walk leading south from Hartland Quay, passes behind St Catherine's Tor and on towards Speke's Mill Mouth. The flat grassy area inland from St Catherine's shows evidence of several low banks once impounding ponds. This may relate to a tradition that Hartland Abbey monks once using the area as a swannery.

My air flight photos were all taken near high tide but the tidal range here is some eight metres, so that at low tide the reefs are exposed as platforms of intricate folds and contortions every bit as impressive as those in the cliffs. Here the low tide shore as seen from St Catherine's Tor.

"....The grandest cliff scenery in the whole area is between Hartland Point and Morwenstow... To the south of Hartland Quay, the grandeur of the rocks laid bare in the cliff by sea erosion, and of the reefs on the shore, almost defies description."
A.E. Newell Arber (1911)

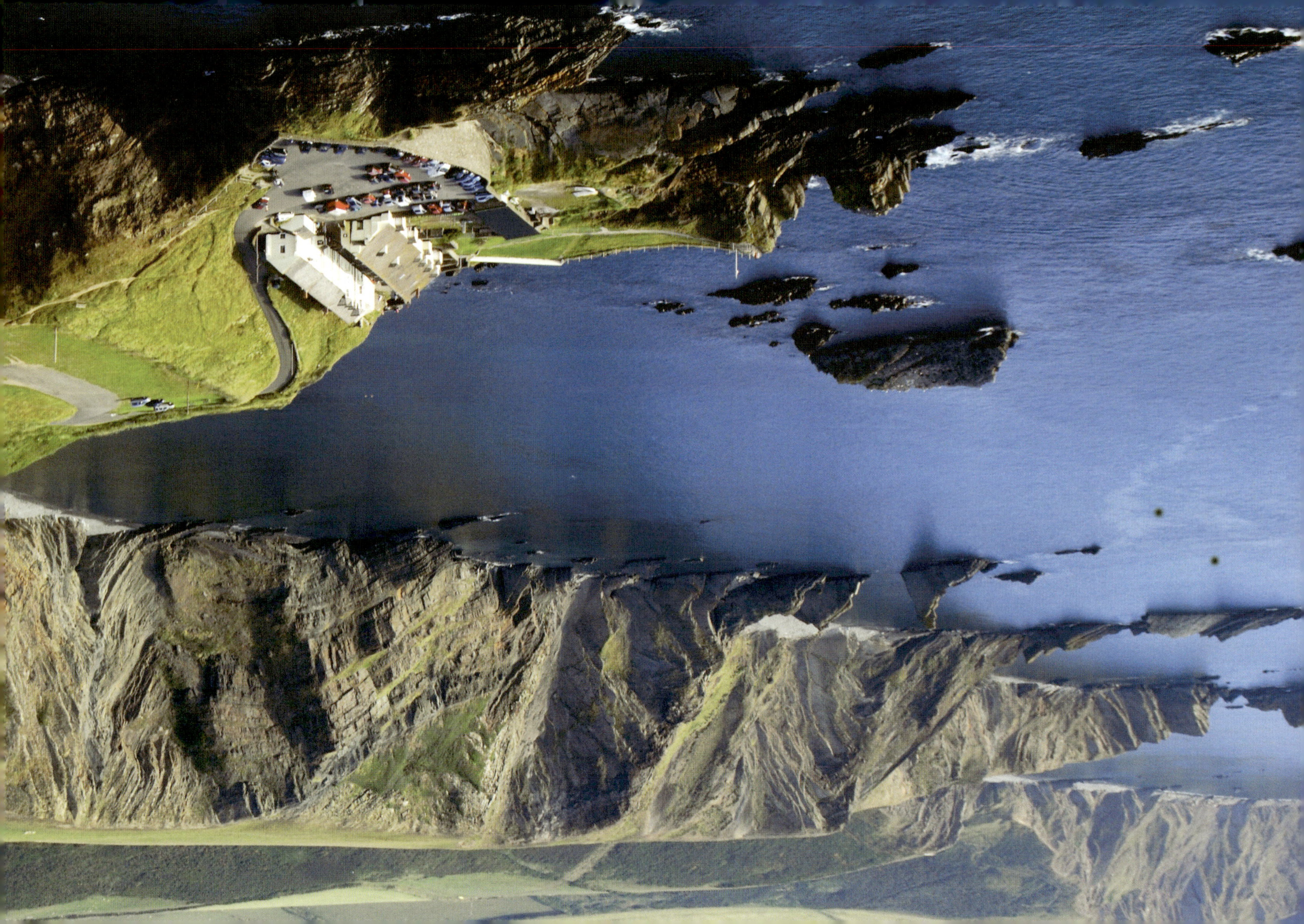

We have reached Hartland Quay. Seen on a midsummer evening, bathed in the warm light of a low sun in a clear sky, and with a calm placid sea, this could be mistaken for the Mediterranean Riviera. Such peace is atypical, for even on calm days a deep swell (from Labrador?) usually heaves and breaks against the rocky shore. Furthermore, being part of the Atlantic wall, this west-facing shore is the first to feel the full fury of the wind-driven waves of Atlantic storms. One of the attractions of the Quay is to stand behind a fence, in safety, yet to face the power of a force eight gale. Thrilled to feel through your feet, the hammer blows of the breaking waves; to lick the salt from your lips, or laughing, to be caught in a sheet of wind-driven spray.

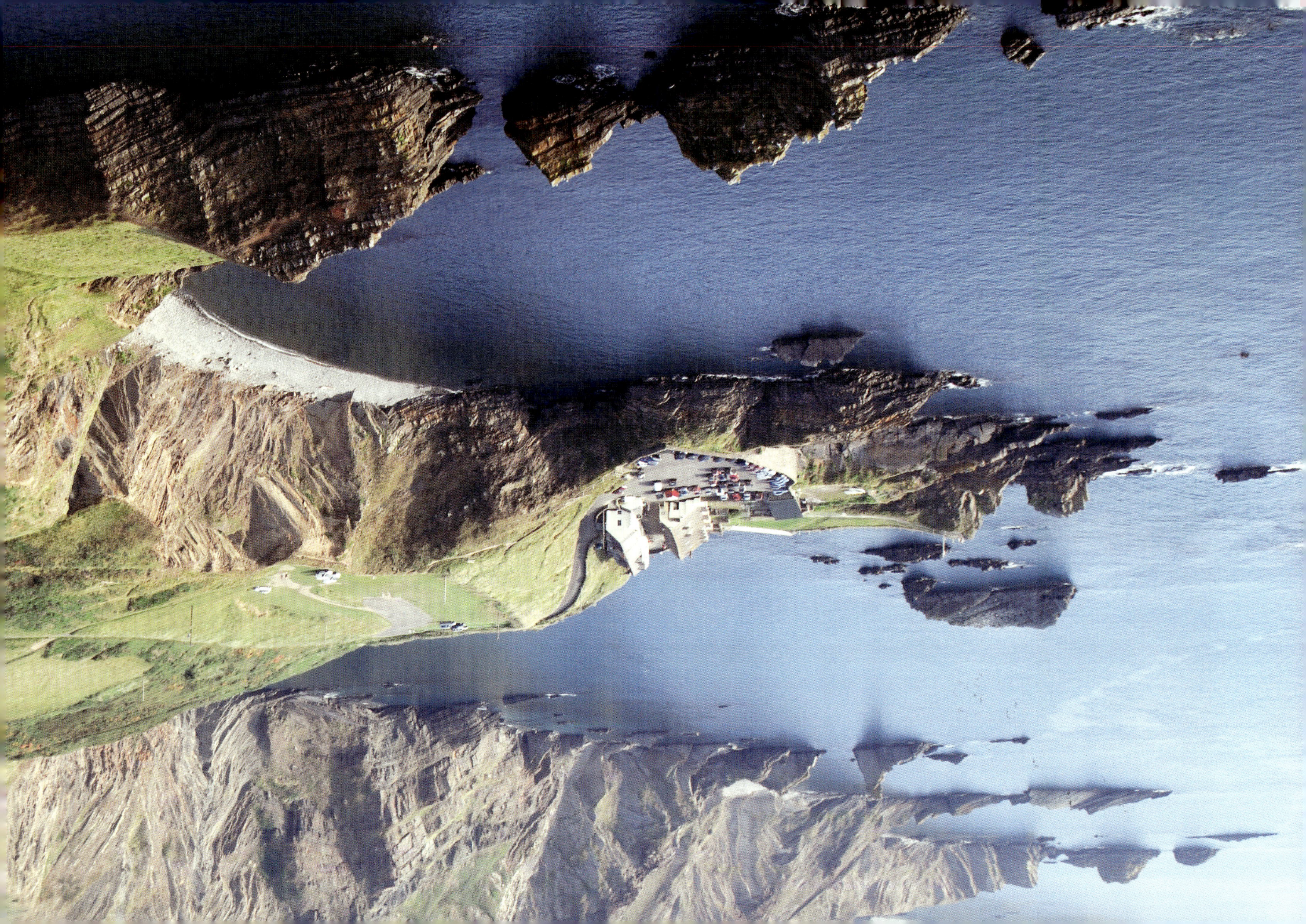

Air photo above: Screda Point is in the foreground and then, beyond Well Beach, is Hartland Quay Hotel. The large isolated rock (above the flagpole viewpoint) is Life Rock. This marks the entrance to the bay which at low tide exposes Warren Beach behind which towers the cliffs of the Warren.

The photo (right) was taken from the lower car park of the hotel looking south to the reef of Screda Point and beyond.

Faced with such a storm I took my photo and then glanced at nearby visitors. They had expressions of horror, even terror but, at the same time, pleasure. This, I took to be the modern equivalent of what was once called the 'sublime' - the elevated feeling experienced by viewers of paintings of disasters or the awesome power of nature, but which, like our visitors, was not actually life-threatening to the observer.

These storms are reminders of the countless wrecks of sailing craft along this coast. How far back does one's empathy stretch for the embayed mariner? One hopes, a long way and yet the relating of an individual experience tugs at the heart most strongly. William Slade, writing in *'Out of Appledore'* (E) recalls an occasion in 1903 when, as a cabin boy on his father's ketch *Alpha*, the ship was struck by a sudden gale off Sharpnose. As the ketch struggled northwards the threatening lee shore got closer until, approaching Hartland Point, William writes; *'Father put his arm round me and his words were full of affection and tragedy, "You'll never see Mother again".'* In this case this was not the end of the story.

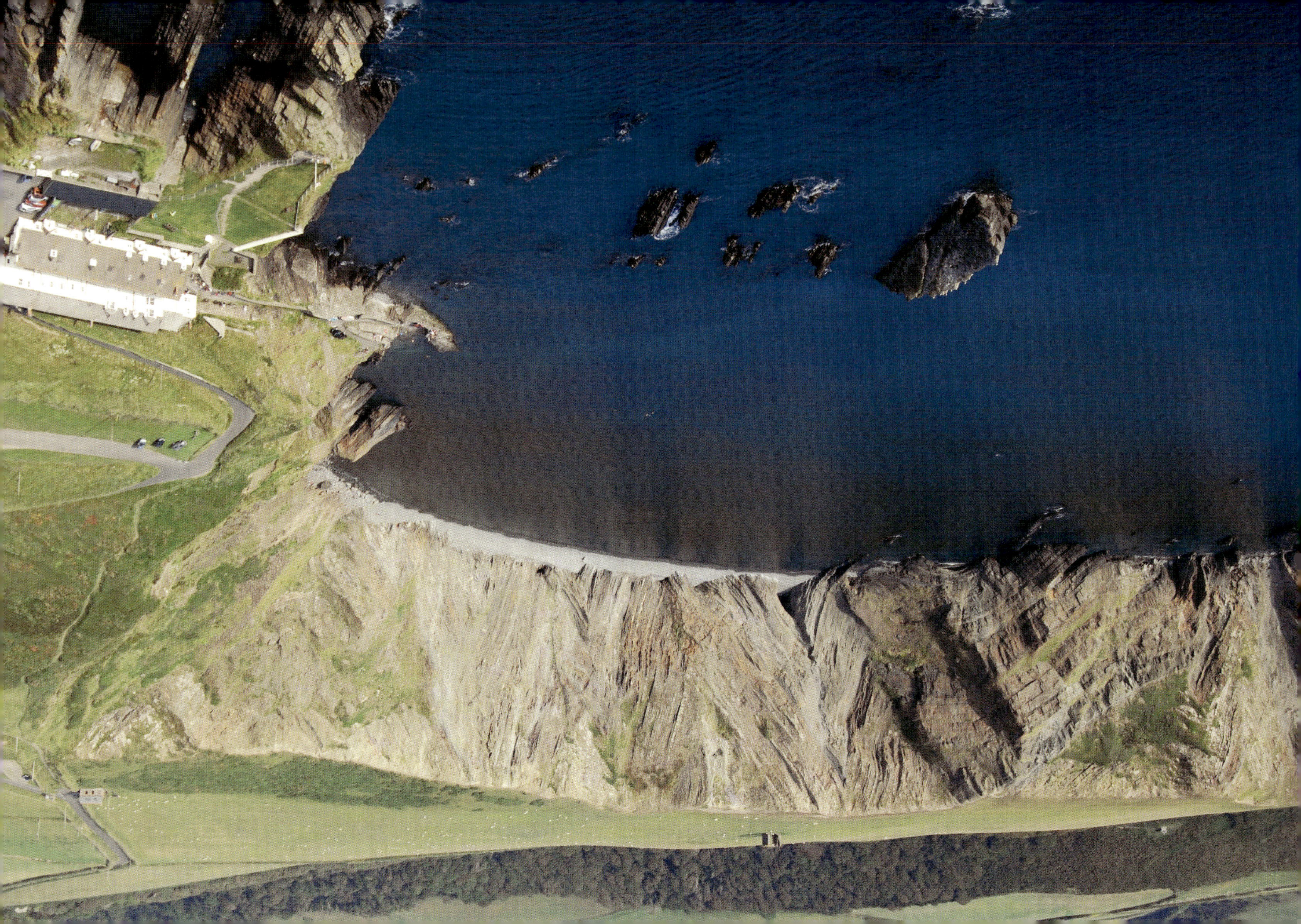

"There was a deep place of water within the bay. So men have thrown out a pier shaped like a human arm to embrace as it were whatsoever vessel may be there. The land clasps the ship to her breast." Rev Stephen Hawker (1805-1875) Parson-poet of Morwenstow.

G 3

Before the end of the 16th century the Hartland Peninsula was a remote neglected corner of Devon, bedevilled by poor, slow and hence expensive land transport hindering trade and development. Furthermore, although sea transport was relatively cheap and fast, there were no safe havens on either side of the Hartland peninsula. A tradition of 'beach work' had developed whereby small sailing craft would land on accessible beaches at high tide, have 12 hours to unload and then refloat on the following tide. However, this was very weather-dependent and a hazardous operation on these rocky shores at all times.

The later part of the 16th century saw an expansion of English maritime trading both overseas and coastwise. Warren Beach took advantage of this growing commercial opportunity as, despite its exposed location, it had relatively easy access inland and a flat area suitable for port facilities in close proximity. In the last years of the 16th century a quay was constructed using the natural rock barrier which connected the shore with Life Rock (see air photo above).

The photo (right), looking across the bay with Life Rock on the extreme left, shows the quay in operation in 1878. Warren Beach, including the harbour floor, dries out at low tide so the tradition of 'beach work' continued to be the norm. The vessel in the photo is being unloaded with coal destined to be taken up to Hartland by donkey cart. Another bulky cargo was limestone from South Wales, which fed the quayside limekiln seen on the right of the photo. The quay not only sheltered these operations from rough seas but also provided a haven for any small craft sheltering from rough seas along this 'iron' coast.

The quay was essentially an expensive but profitable commercial venture and flourished for over 200 years. However, road improvements, the arrival of the railway in Bideford (1855), a long agricultural depression in the 19th century and alternative sources of cheap lime, meant that it was no longer economic to make the constant, expensive repairs necessary to counter the ravages of the sea. Storm damage in 1887 and again in 1896 eventually spelt the end to what had already become a commercial liability. Today, remains of the quay can be seen as a scatter of huge stone blocks covering the former harbour floor. Most of the building associated with the harbour facilities have survived, albeit with a change in function.

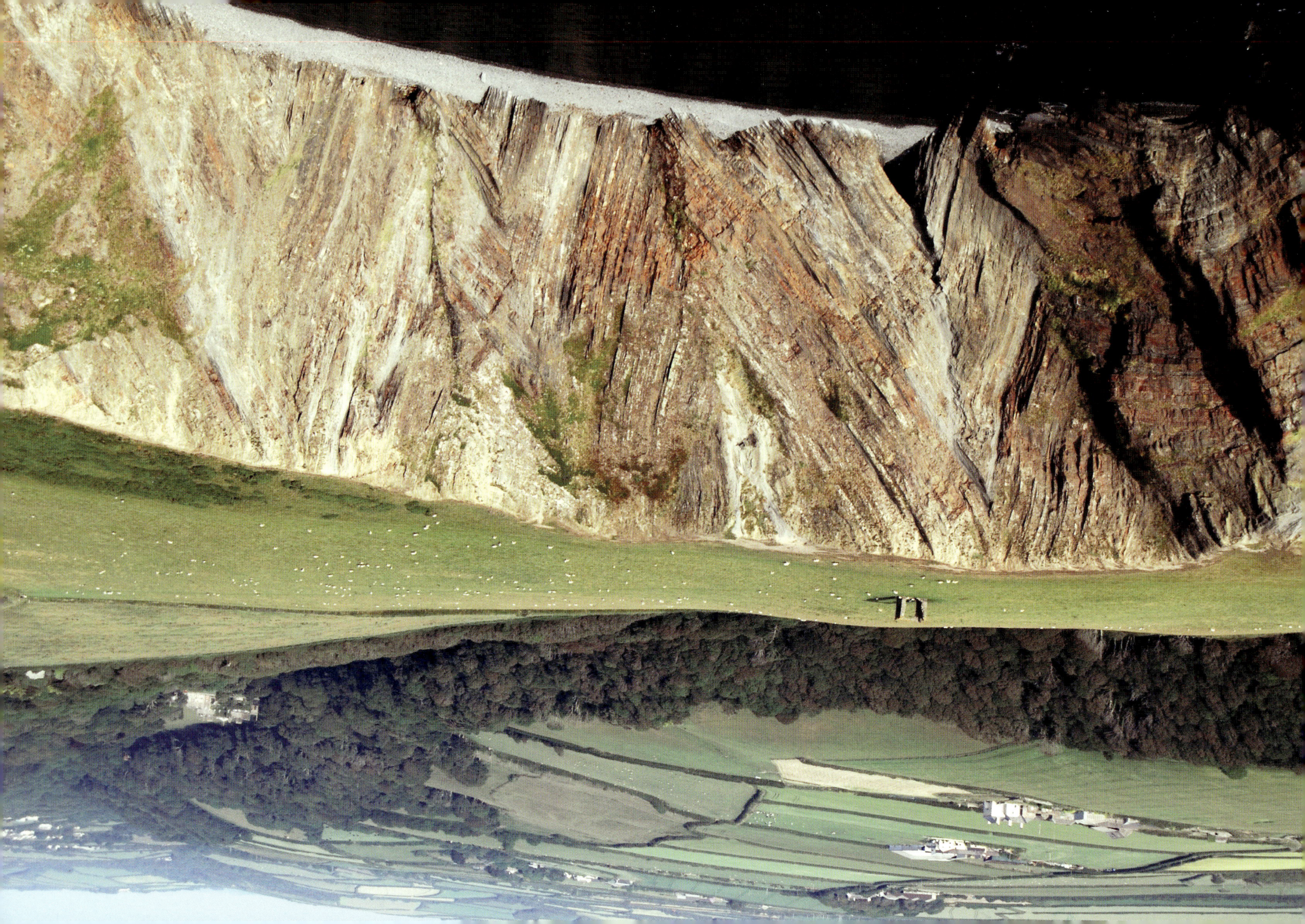

Warren Beach at high (above) and low (below) water. The cliffs give a striking visual representation of the fearsome power of the effects of continental collision. However, do not become too overcome with feelings of the 'sublime' by venturing too close to the cliff foot without a helmet, as these cliffs can, without warning, shed loose blocks of rock. The cliff-top ruin was probably orginally a Medieval Warrener's House, located centrally to guard the rabbit warren, a valued resource in those days. Later it became a summer house and a romantic ruin locally known as 'The Pleasure House' (use unknown!). Through the arch in the ruin is seen the tower of Stoke Church about a half-mile inland. The tower is a prominent landscape feature for many miles around. The other small photo shows the same tower with standing stone, viewed from the hill adjacent to St Catherine's Tor. Unlike Stoke, Hartland Abbey, originally founded as a monastery in the 12th century, nestles within the valley of the Abbey River.

Hartland Quay is such a wonderful open air geological demonstration laboratory that it attracts student groups from far and wide. Non-specialist visitors too are fascinated by the magnificent cliffs and seek some straightforward explanation for the folded rocks and their history. There is no way that on our rapid fly past we could satisfy either audience. However, in this case we can recommend a solution that admirably fills the bill. *Geology at Hartland Quay* by Chris Cornford and Alan Childs (**4**) introduces a walk along this beach providing a booklet at both levels of commentary. This is achieved by addressing each audience on alternating pages throughout the booklet and it works well.

4.　3.

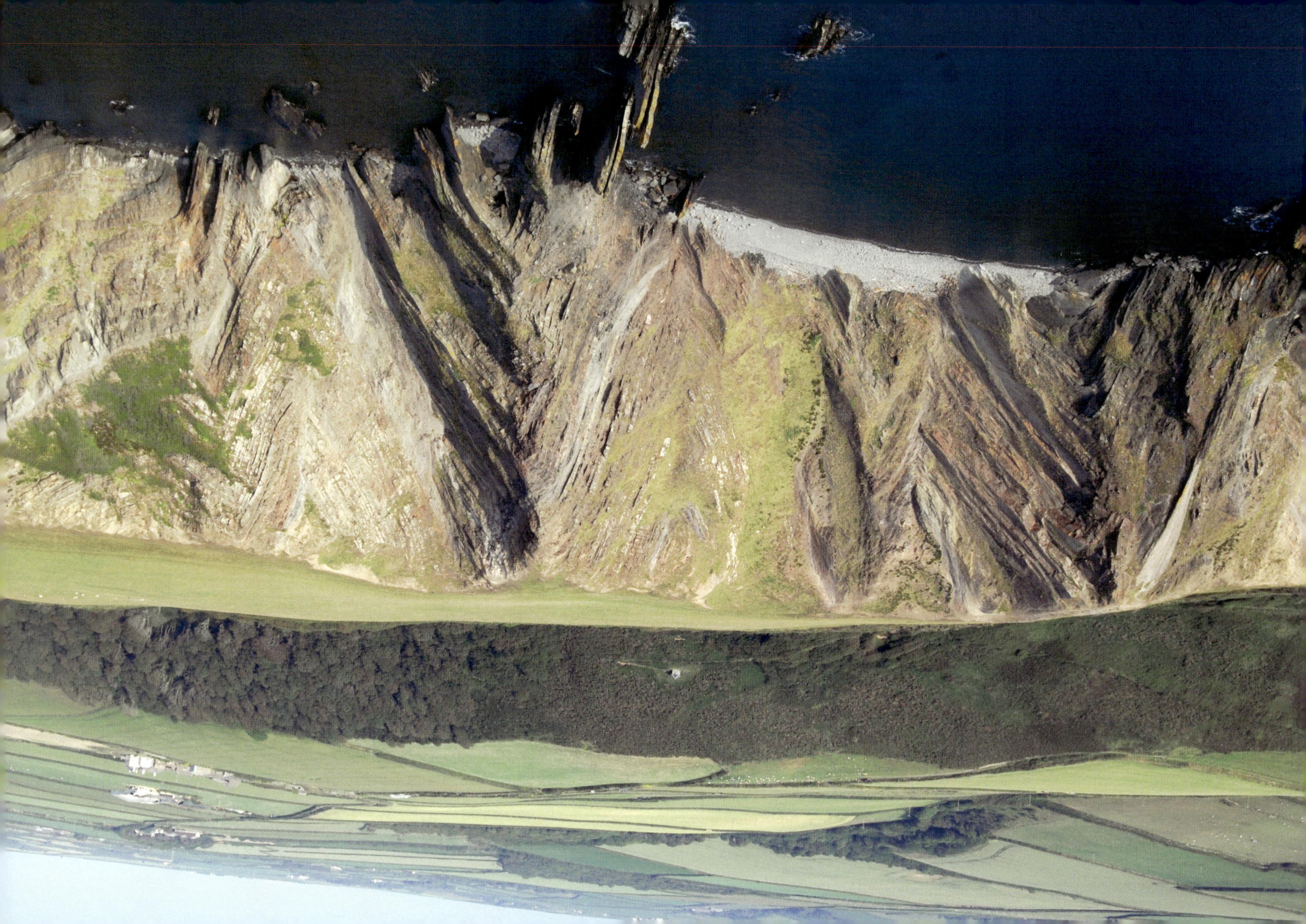

Broad Beach and the cliffs which back it, are really a continuation of Warren Beach and to some may look a bit too similar! - A case of ABC? When I was on an escorted tour of historic churches in Sicily, eventually even the most hardened tourists were reduced to 'Another Bloody Church'. Well, this time let us look down on what is exposed at low tide. The waves have scythed a giant step cut into the coastal landscape. The exposed shore platform is the tread of this step whilst the cliffs are the riser (the back of the step), created by land tumbling into the sea as, at high tide, the waves work relentlessly to remove the land's support. So, the rocks of the rocky shore are the same as the cliffs but viewed in plan instead of section.

You can usually trace a bed of rock down the cliff and then, after disappearing briefly from view beneath the storm beach, it re-emerges and can be followed out across the wave-cut platform towards low tide. Plenty of questions one might ask about all that and perhaps its too simple a statement, but tracing the route of beds or folds, or noting where the beds are dislocated by a fault, are sound steps in the observation of detail (a field sketch?) which are often necessary to advance one's understanding of a landscape be it as an artist or scientist. Discuss with reasons? Well, I cannot look down on this shore without a surge of pleasure. Where does that pleasure come from?

1 3 4

Broad Beach

Warren Beach

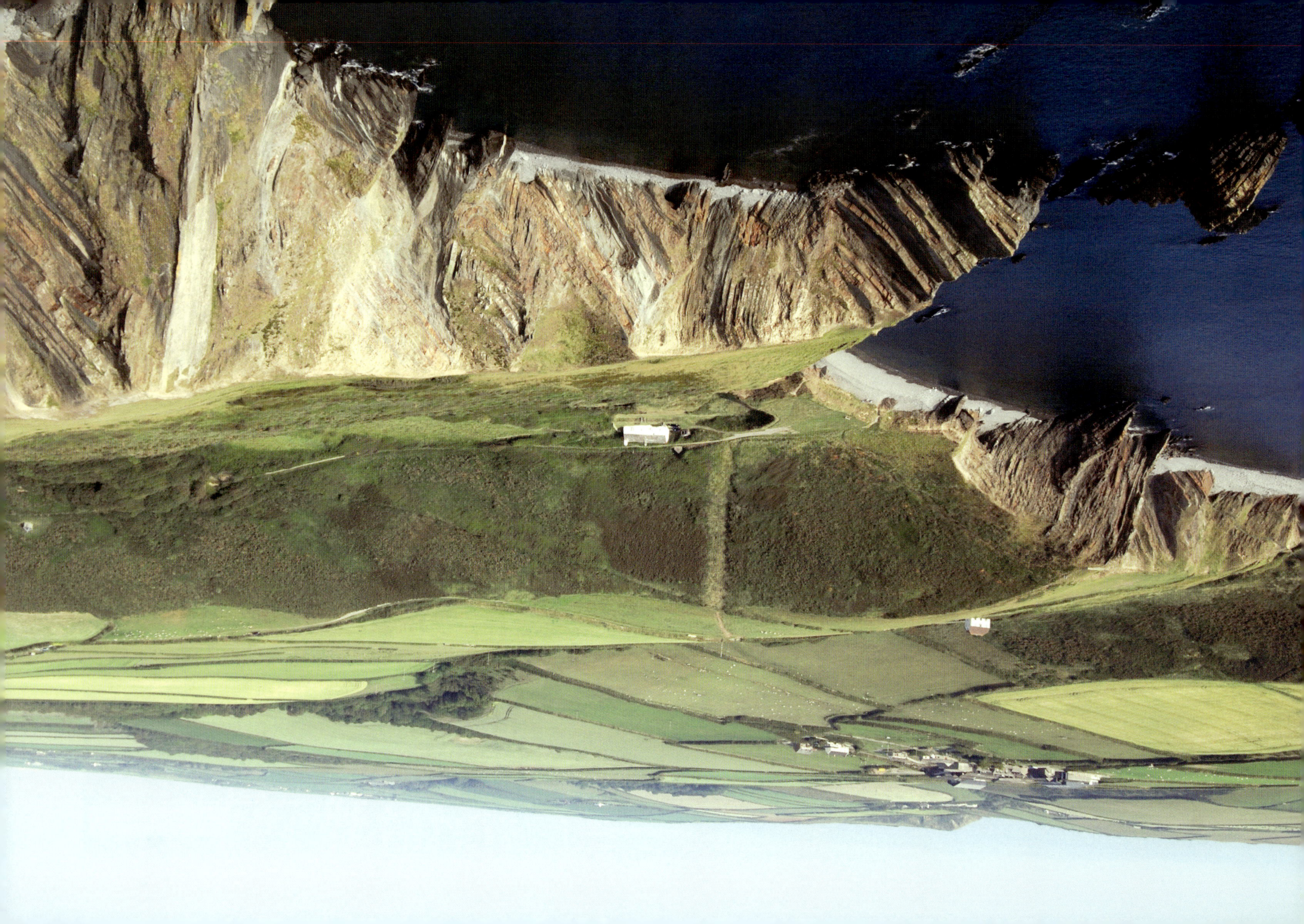

Abbey River and Blackpool Mill

The entrenched Abbey River reaches the sea at Blackpool Mill in a short, steep-sided gorge. Most of the coombes seen in these air photos can be traced inland by the meandering threads of their uncultivated valley sides. Where sheltered from the wind-driven salt spray, these slopes are clothed in conspicuous dark green, deciduous woodland. The settlement on the hill is Blegberry, a farm surrounded by a fortified wall with loop holes and and observation platform. It was built in 1627, and now, perhaps for a small parcel of time, its defences are unnecessary. The photo (left below) was taken circa 1967 and little in the landscape has changed since then. The amphitheatre-like curved cliff just seawards from the cottage is where the river once meandered, cutting deep into the former valley floor, now left as a flat tableland between the meander cliff and the sea.

Sitting at home in Oxfordshire in 2008 watching the BBC television drama of 'Sense and Sensibility', we, like many people in North-West Devon, suddenly jumped as we recognised the Barton Cottage that Mrs Dashwood moved to with her three daughters on the death of her husband was in fact Blackpool Mill. I turned to my copy of the book (Chapter VI) and recognised why this delightfully remote spot could serve that purpose so well.

> *"It was a pleasant fertile spot, well wooded, and rich in pasture. After winding along it for more than a mile, they reached their own house. A small green court was the whole of its demesne in front; and a neat wicket gate admitted them into it. … As a house, Barton Cottage, though small, was comfortable and compact; but as a cottage it was defective, for the building was regular, the roof was tiled, the window shutters were not painted green, nor were the walls covered with honeysuckles….The situation of the house was good. High hills rose immediately behind, and at no great distance on each side; some of which were open downs, the others cultivated and woody…. The prospect in front was more extensive; it commanded the whole of the valley, and reached into the country beyond."* (Jane Austen; 'Sense and Sensibility').

In a field photograph and notebook, kept by the Bideford geologist Inkermann Rogers, I found a postcard of this site (right) taken from the other side of the stream. The notebook was dated 1907 but the photo was a postcard and might have been taken some years earlier. I was intrigued, for in the foreground, next to the bridge which crosses the stream, is a roofless building. Unlike the Marsland Mouth Mill, 'Blackpool Mill' did not appear to have an obvious feed leat. I did wonder if the ruin was perhaps the remains of a Grist Mill referred to in earlier estate maps. If so its site would suggest an undershot waterwheel fed directly from the stream, perhaps augmented by a holding pond immediately upstream? Enquiries in Hartland were interesting but inconclusive and so, at the time of writing, I just leave this as an open question.

H 3

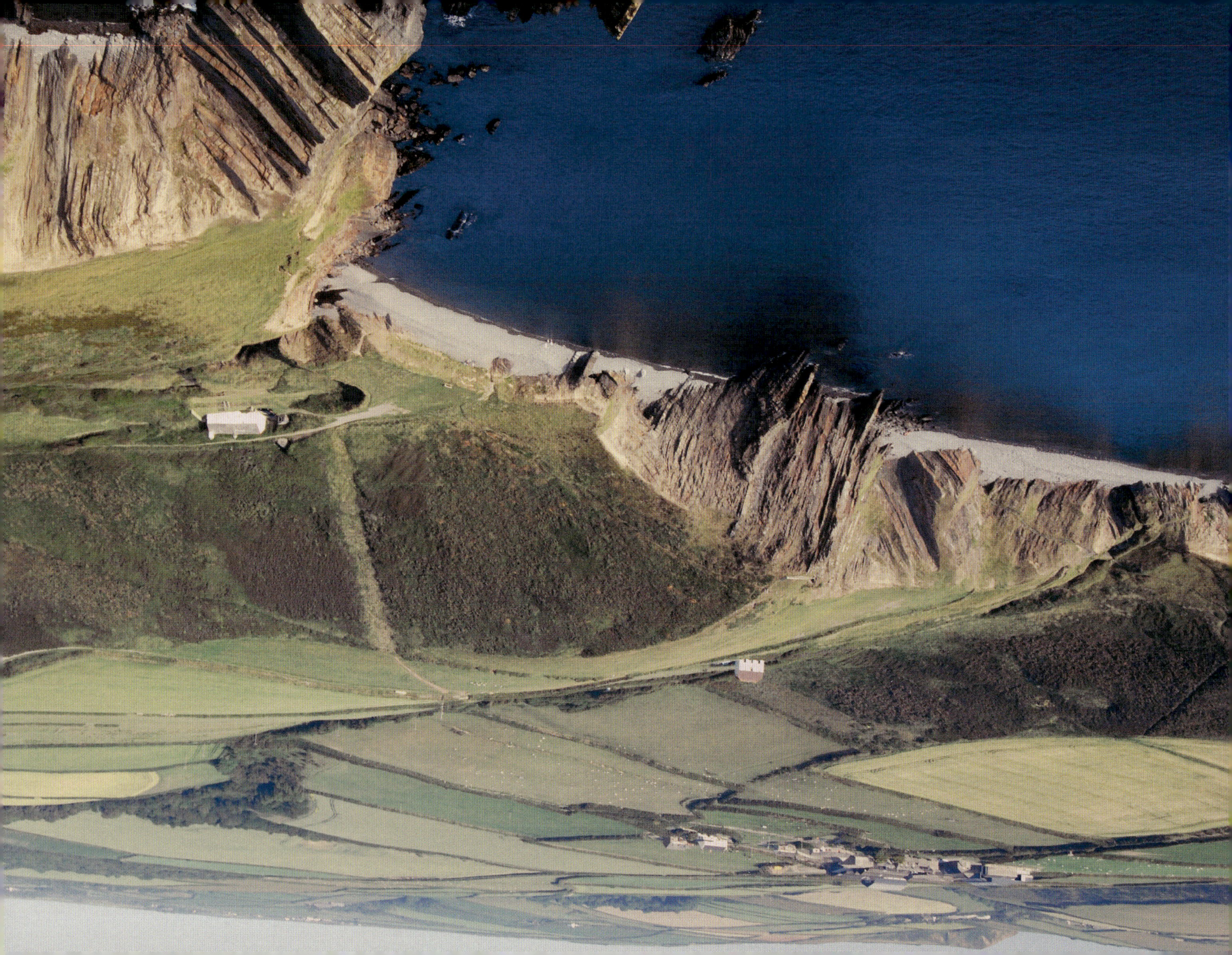

Reefs   In my air photos of this coast, high tide obscures the plethora of sawtoothed reefs which leap seawards until, eventually they are swallowed in crashing surf-smoke. My father was interested in the juxtaposition of agitation or fluid movement against the calm of solid presence, in this case (sketch below, top left) waves and solid rock. My photos often seem to reflect this too. I would like to think there was some cross fertilisation going on but I may have just been unconsciously absorbing the wisdom of my father.

1   3   4

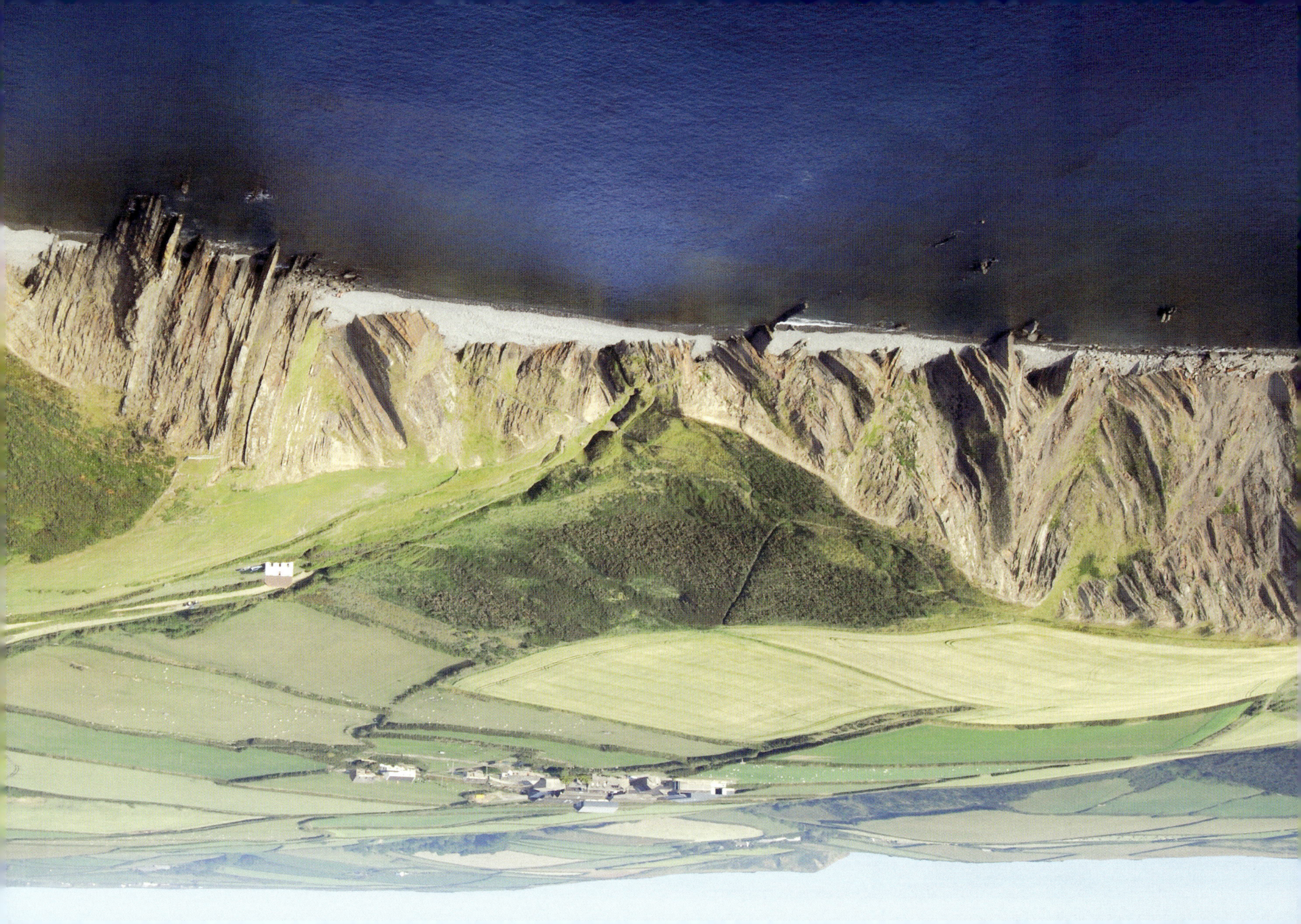

Berry Cliff Above: Just north of Blackpool Mill is Berry Cliff and Blegberry Beach seen here at a calm high tide. Below: As the tide recedes, the familiar pattern of seaward probing reefs is exposed. In the background is Damehole Point, always a significant headland to be treated with caution when kayaking along this coast close inshore.

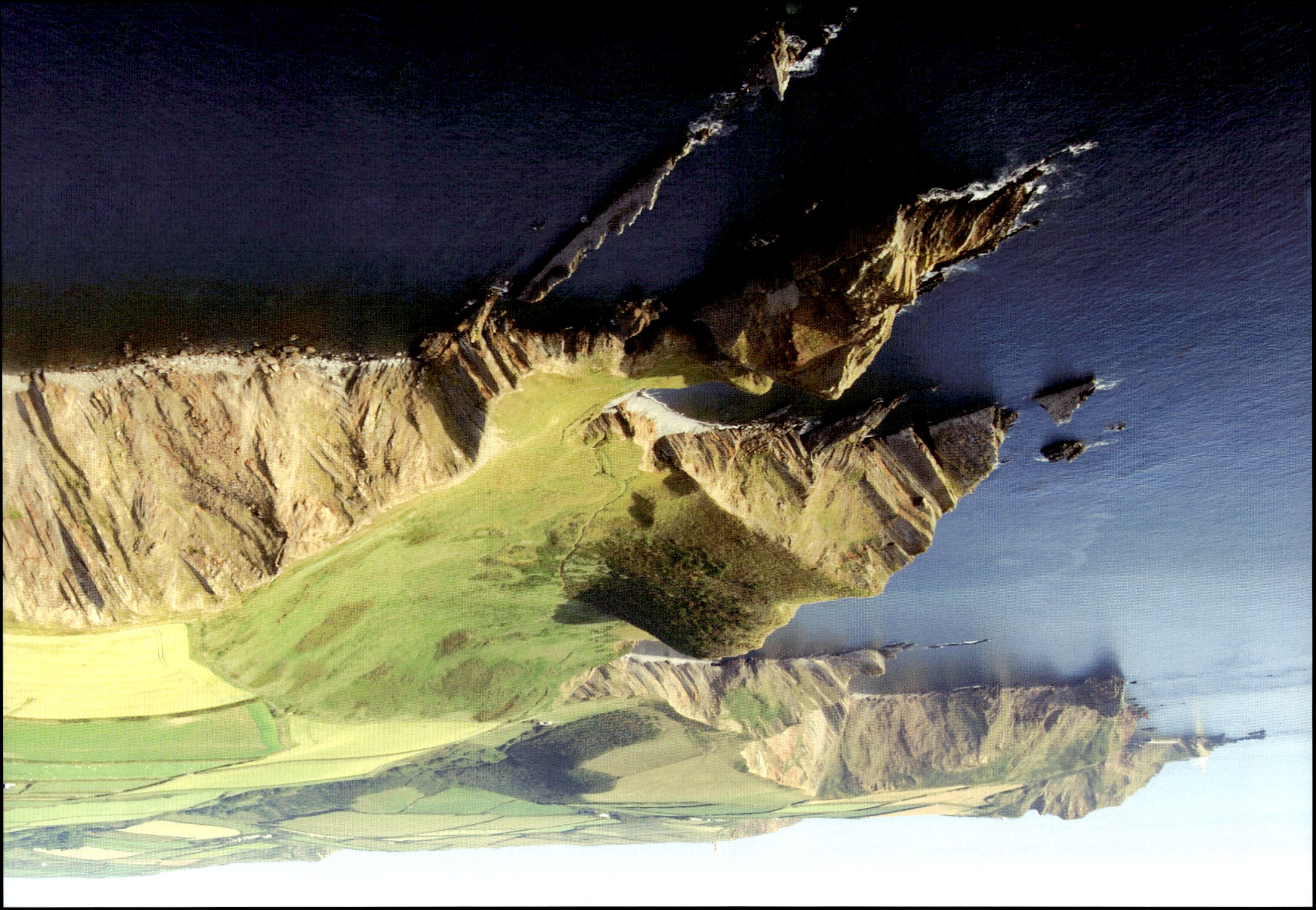

Damehole Point is highest on its seaward side and dips landwards, separated from higher land eastwards by a low swathe of grass called **Smoothlands**. This is the dry former lower course of the Titchberry Water, the coombe you can see in the distance with its dark tree-lined valley sides tracing its valley inland from the sea. At some time in the comparatively recent past, erosion of the local cliffs by the sea has breached the valley side, capturing the stream and leaving the 'dry' beheaded valley of Smoothlands beyond and leaving the Titchberry Water to tumble over the cliff edge onto the beach below.

A 1 3

...at the northern extremity of Smoothlands, the sea has cut out certain beds of the limb of a syncline, and left curved reefs of sandstones, projecting like the ribs of some large wreck stranded on the shore. These afford excellent illustrations of how the sea works at the rocks of a cliff, cutting out the softer beds, and slowly eroding the harder sandstones. (Newell Arber 1911)

To wander through Smoothlands in May is a breathtaking experience, a wild flower meadow of scent and sight. What most of these flowers have in common, that gives them a distinct advantage in this environment, is a tolerance to salt-laden winds which lash this coast in winter. Thrift (Sea pinks), white-flowered Sea Campion and Rock Samphire can survive even on the exposed seaward slopes and most can be found in abundance along much of this coast.

*And down on knees aright I me set,
And as I could this fresh flow'r I grette.
Kneeling always till it enclosed was
Upon the small, and soft, sweete gras.*
(Geoffrey Chaucer. c1343 - 1400).

52

Smoothlands   Damehole Point

It was on the Hartland coast that I really learnt my coastal sea kayaking, nearly always solo, but just once or twice with a companion, providing good company and the occasional personal photographic record.

It is a thrilling coast both visually and for the feel of the sea but, as I have emphasised in my introduction, a good sandy shore is where you should take your first solo sea lessons.

I have always kept a kayaking log, sometimes translated into an annotated map of the day's experiences. Other experiences and feelings I write up in a Commonplace book, a sort of scrapbook of notes, descriptions, experiences and appreciated quotes made by other people. My written jottings, for me, revive personal experiences better than photographs. I have kept just such a book ever since discovering Robert Southey's 'Commonplace book' (1799), where he describes his visit to the Valley of Rocks, Lynton.

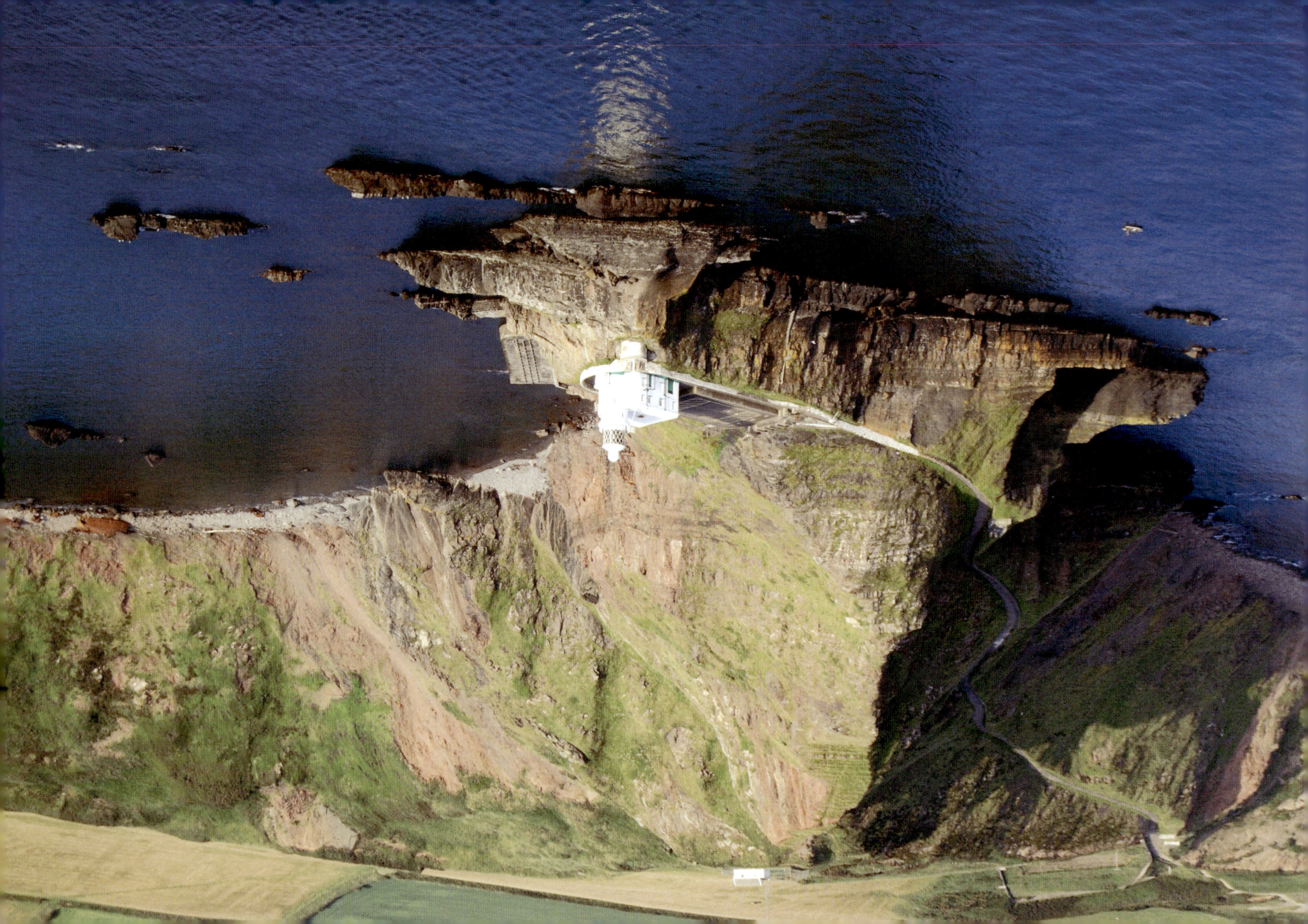

Hartland Point (the Roman Promontory of Hercules?). Established in 1874, the lighthouse was constructed on a large rock right at the end of the promontory. Unanticipated erosion of this rock eventually necessitated concrete sea defences to reinforce the base of the rock. The light was automated in 1984, prior to which there were four keepers, all living on site, together with their families. The house is now in private hands.

Left: We were lucky having a calm sunny evening for our photographic flight, yet a more memorable experience is perhaps to visit the point during a storm when from the cliff top you lean into an eye-watering gusty gale.

On 31 December 1982 the MS Johanna, carrying a cargo of wheat from Holland to Cardiff, was driven by such a gale onto rocks just south of the lighthouse. A Chivenor helicopter rescued four of the crew. Three officers were later taken off by the RNLI lifeboat from Clovelly. The last rusting remains of the hull can still be seen in the photo above.

Right: January 1983. A field sketch of the Johanna, sent to me in Oxford by my father, Joe Keene.

Left: By the time I visited the wreck at the end of March 1983 the Johanna had broken in two, but it remains a point of interest for visitors to this day.

If you visit these cliffs frequently it is interesting to plot the gradual disintegration of each wreck. Sometimes, however, the curve of a heavy robust boiler, glimpsed at low tide, is the only sign left of a past catastrophe.

The inner passage

Hartland Point

With a tidal range of some eight metres in Bideford Bay the tidal race around Hartland Point is quite spectacular. Here (right) the white water of the outgoing tide is sweeping around the point. A shallow reef, Tense Rocks, lies just off shore and in its time, particularly before the lighthouse, these rocks were responsible for many wrecks.

15.04.1974: Kayak. Hartland Quay to Westward Ho!
"I have done this 18-mile trip on a number of occasions and never tire of it, always kayaked this way round, as Hartland Point is only two miles north of the quay and so I can keep my options open and easily turn back if it looks too choppy. Over breakfast at Westward Ho! where it may be calm and sunny, I can never be sure of the same for Hartland. Sometimes it is rougher than I anticipate. If I don't like what I see I always have the option of turning south towards Welcombe. Sometimes the Hartland coast is under a blanket of coastal fog.

I always try to navigate Hartland Point on slack water at high tide thus avoiding the tide race which here brushes close to the shore. What brought safety so forcefully to mind this morning was that from the cliffs above the quay I saw the smudgy line of white horses where the tide spills over Tense Rocks, a shallow reef just off-shore from the headland.

Eighteen miles to home. The waterproof map is secure under elastic straps on the foredeck; whistle and compass attached to the uninflated life jacket. Pasties, apples, notebook and my camera, a Voigtlander Vito B, packed into my waterproof ammunition box. Also in the box are matches, chalk, pencil, paper, tin opener, string, two pence, a pound note, safety pin, Elastoplast, water purifying tablets, a spare whistle, a tube of Bostik, carpet tape, a candle, a bottle opener, two sachets of instant coffee and two of coffee-mate.

Concocting and unnecessarily refining and modifying this emergency pack was the delight of several cold winter evenings, lazing on the rug in front of a log fire, living instant high adventure as the necessity of each item was pondered. Two cans of beer needing no such protection are pushed down.

Spray-deck on, I knuckle the kayak into the shallows and I am away. I keep inshore amongst the rocks. The tide and sea are both with me. However, it's a switchback ride seawards and where will it take me? I play safe and ride the swell as close to the shore as I dare. It may look horrendous in photos but with a very shallow draught and keeping an eye on the wave troughs ahead, most of the hidden rocks close enough to the surface to be a danger, give themselves away with little swirls in the wave troughs. I've had no catastrophe on that score so far." (from log)

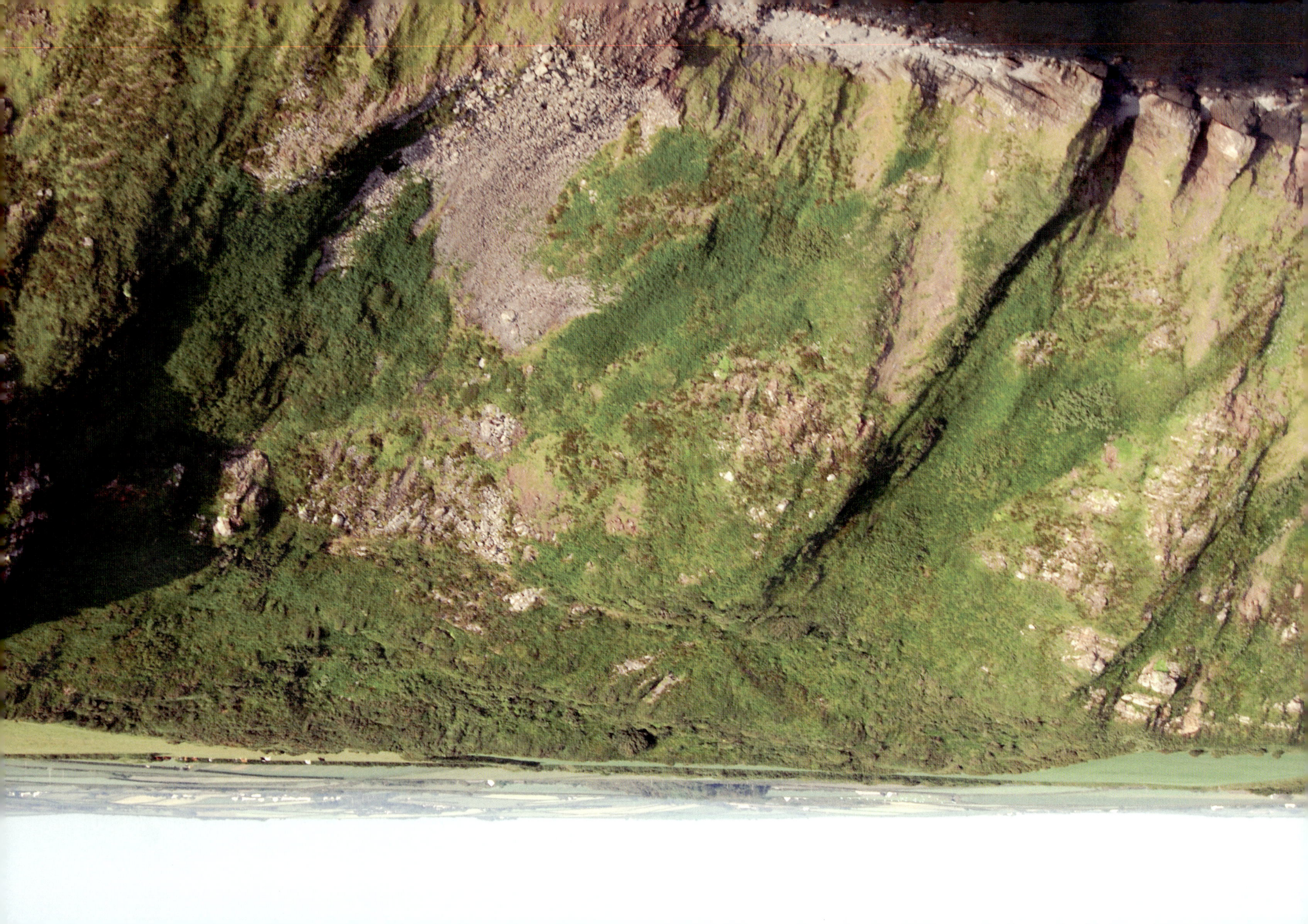

Around Hartland Point.

"With no one to talk to, confidence strangely ebbs and flows with little apparent logic. A sea which frightens me to a standstill may, a few minutes later, appear an exciting challenge. What value then the judgement that sends me round this choppy point?

Beyond Upright Cliff, the lighthouse, in clean Trinity House black and white, stands against the headland with Victorian assurance. From the lighthouse a restless white ribbon runs along the horizon. The black slab of Lundy lies 'hull-down' twelve miles out in the Bristol Channel, but its black cliffs rise straight from the jumping line of sea now barely a quarter of a mile ahead.

I have mistimed it. The flood tide is still running but not too strongly I think. Should I wait for the slack? In an 'exciting challenge' moment I decide that rather than hang around I will go for it.

Sharp rocks are to hand. Seawards the white leaping peaks of the race offer no passage, but I have a card up my sleeve, for between a long sea-washed reef and the lighthouse shore there is, at high tide, a narrow lead of water, an inner passage which can take the edge off the tugging tide and subdue the following swell. Well, I've done it before and that's what I will do I thought. However, today waves surge violently down the passage.

No good having a 'frightened to a standstill' moment now for I am committed to the channel before my craning neck can be sure that safe waters lie beyond.

Half surfing on a green wave, paddles digging, shoulders strong, fighting the yaw, I sort of influenced my passage as I roared down the passage. I can't say I was fully in control but rather was spat out suddenly into the comparatively calm water at the entrance to Barley Bay. First, a rising bubble of glee, then a reawakening to the world beyond my paddles and the realisation that that was a close run thing."

Turning the point from the Atlantic side of the peninsula into Bideford Bay is reflected in a dramatic change of scenery. The cliff top plateaux are still there and, although invisible from a kayak, are well displayed from the air. However, the reefs, which on the Atlantic side ran discordantly out into the sea, now lie parallel to the cliffs, providing close passage beneath sloping walls of wildly vegetated cliffs with greenery often reaching down to the shore.

The stretch of coast from Hartland Point to Bucks Mills generally faces away from the Atlantic storms and salt-laden gales and although Atlantic waves reach the coast they are commonly bent (refracted) around Hartland Point, losing some of their power. Storm waves that strike this coast are at their maximum efficiency from winds blowing across the Bristol Channel from Wales. Everything is relative but it is apparent that this side of the peninsula is more sheltered than the Atlantic coast.

"Barley Bay and Shipload Bay (right) with pocket sized beaches cupped by high cliffs, are tempting stops with good sheltered landing on small cobbles at high tide, but a watery sun and sudden cold fingers of wind push me on.

The kayak slips silently along below damp cliffs, but I disturb gulls which clamour over my progress. The herring gulls are content to wheel high with cacophonous screams, but the quieter fulmars sweep lower, making close passes at the kayak, part inspection, part intimidation. In Scotland, I have even had a skua parting my hair! At high tide, denied their feeding grounds, oystercatchers, curlews, small gulls and a lone heron standing aloof from the jockeying mob below him, wait on the storm beach for the fall of the tide. Disturbed by my close passage, eventually a 'kleep, kleep' of oystercatchers take to the air." (from log)

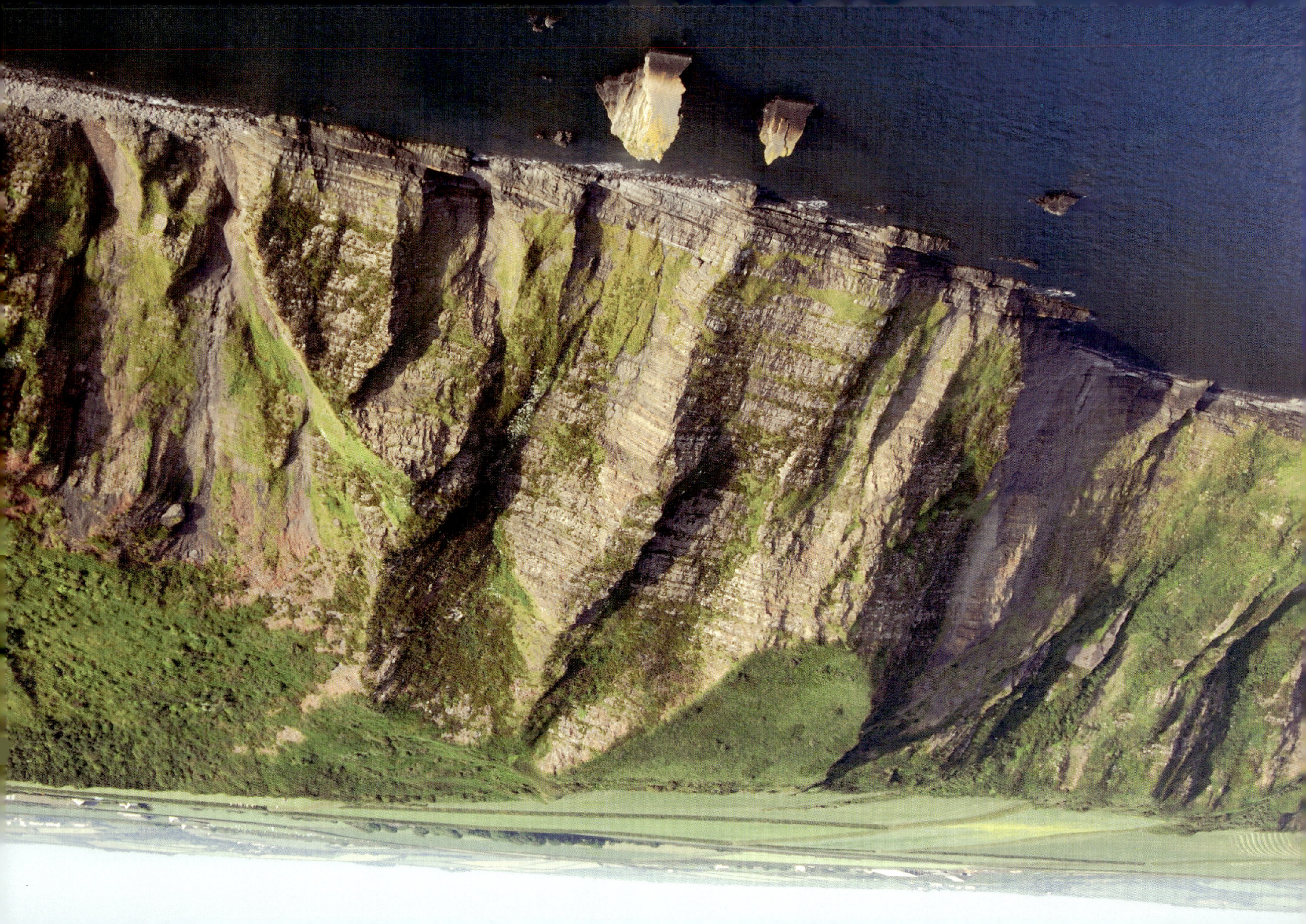

Chapman Rock and Little Chapman Rock (a little geology)

These two stacks on the wave-cut platform and the cliffs of Exmansworthy and Fatacott behind them, illustrate how the different direction (axes) of rock folding between the Atlantic side and the Bideford Bay side of the peninsula dramatically affect the scenery.

On the Atlantic coast the axes of the folds come straight out of the cliff-line with beds thus running out to sea, more or less at right angles to the shore. This results in the frequent reefs running seawards which we have previously noted.

On the Bideford side, the compass direction of the folds has not changed but the direction of the coast has, so that along this stretch of shore the axes of the folds are roughly parallel to the coast, as beds dip either inland or towards the sea.

The stacks here (at high tide) represent the surviving visible remnants of the seaward steeply dipping eastward limb of a fold. The 140-metre cliff face exposes the western limb of the fold dipping steeply inland.

Upper right: At low tide the shore platform is exposed and the stacks stand high and dry but it is difficult to pick out the crest of the fold on the wave-cut platform.

Another feature profoundly influencing the appearance of this stretch of the coast is the large number of coastal landslips. This too seems closely related to the direction of the shore in relation to the axes of the folds. Where the beds dip landwards, away from the sea, the cliff will be particularly susceptible to 'toppling failure'. The sea, undermining the supporting rock base at sea level, causes beds to topple outwards. A mantle of coarse scree is created under a steep cliff at the back of the slip. Where exposed beds within a fold dip seawards, these can be susceptible to the mass movement of rock sliding towards the shore. All these cliff failures will create scars which, even when re-vegetated, will mark the activity of past landslips for many years to come.

Lower right: Immediately to the west of Chapman Rock (towards Hartland Point) is this impressive landslip with obvious attempts to stabilise the movement. The bulging toe of the slip has already been attacked by the sea, removing much of the smaller loose debris. The photo was in taken in 2009. It would be interesting to see what it looks like now.

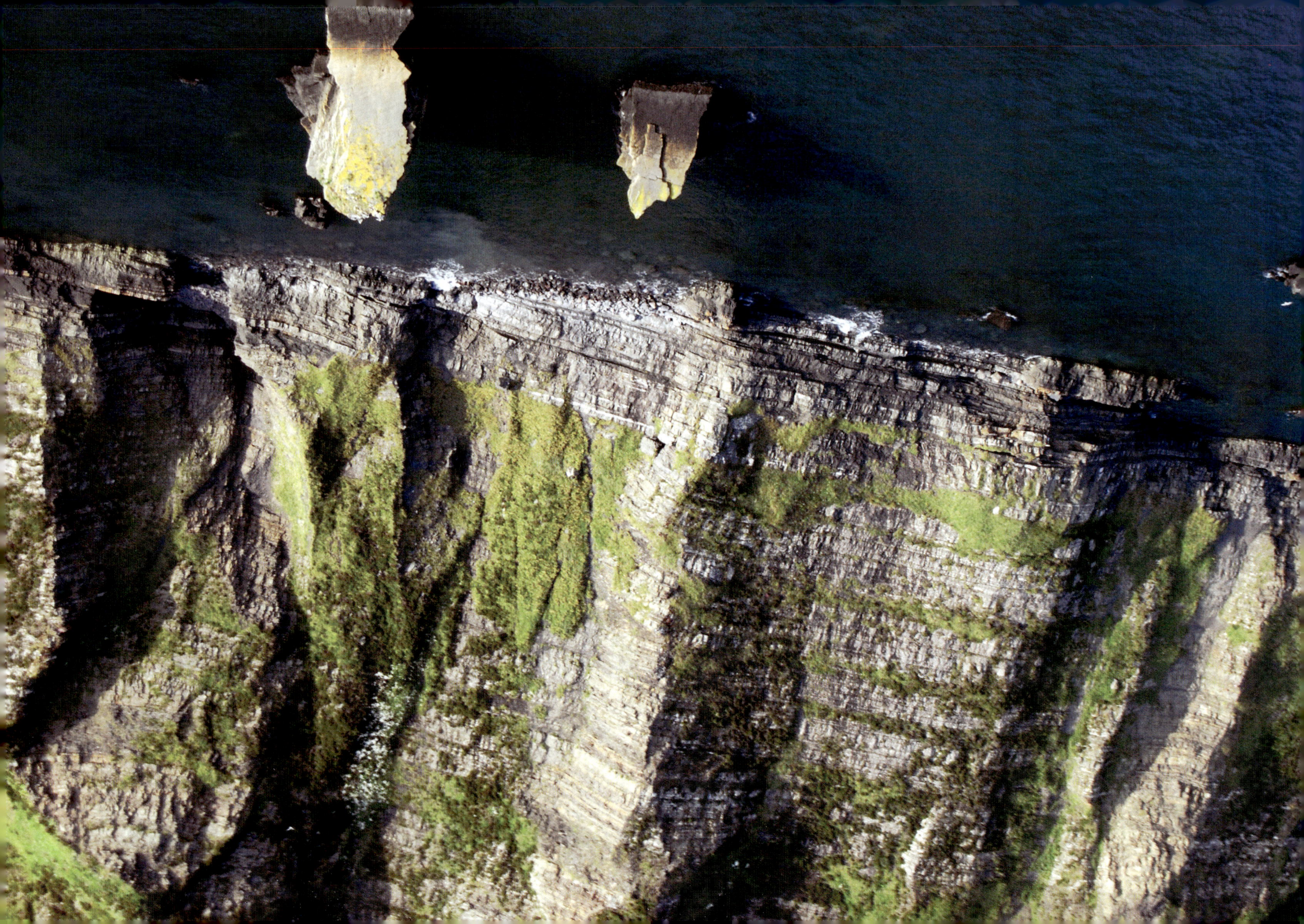

In May 1977 I bought a fibreglass version of a Greenland (Inuit) kayak. It is 18 feet long and with a round bilge and low deck, 'Nordkapp' was 'neutral to windage' staying on course regardless of wind direction - great. It was energy efficient, so easy to paddle at cruising speed for hours. It also had features which were very useful for the North Devon coast - a raised bow and stern to ride over small ice flows and a flat rear deck on which the seal catch of the day could be secured. It was a snug fit. It think it was only £50 because the owner could no longer get into it.

"From the Nordkapp off Clovelly after a straight run across the bay from Westward Ho! Then turned north-west to Chapman Rock (far distance) via Gallant Rock and Blackchurch Rock.

Landed for lunch on Chapman Rock and sat watching the sea and birds before returned to Westward Ho! cruising beneath the cliffs in the late afternoon and evening. A brilliant day."
(from my log)

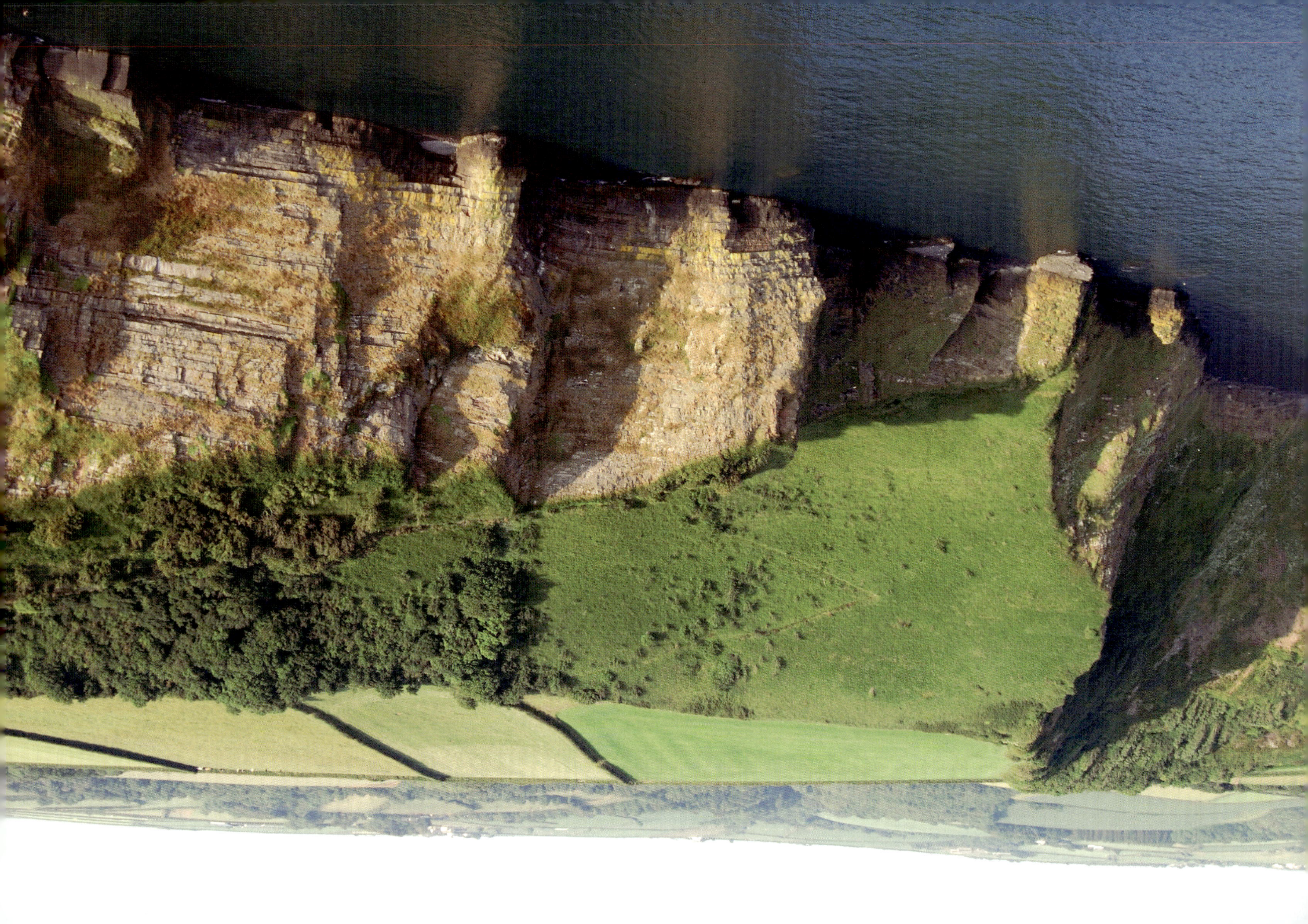

Above: **Beckland Water** below **Windbury Hill**, hangs above the sea.
Left: At times I have delighted in the cool spray of falling fresh-water from coastal waterfalls.

"A hint of sun coincides with reaching Beckland Bay after crossing straight from Westward Ho!. Landing on this wide yet enclosed cove, I felt a surge of satisfaction linked to the physical effort involved. A neoprene wet-suit for these longer exposed runs keeps you warm and wet but sweaty. If the landing is remote enough, the first priority is to strip and go straight for the sea which, after the trip, always feels buttock-clenching cold." (from log)

I turned up this self-portrait (right) after searching through my archives. It felt good, although when, at 77, I went to a full length mirror to compare. The only word I could come up with was "Ozymandias".

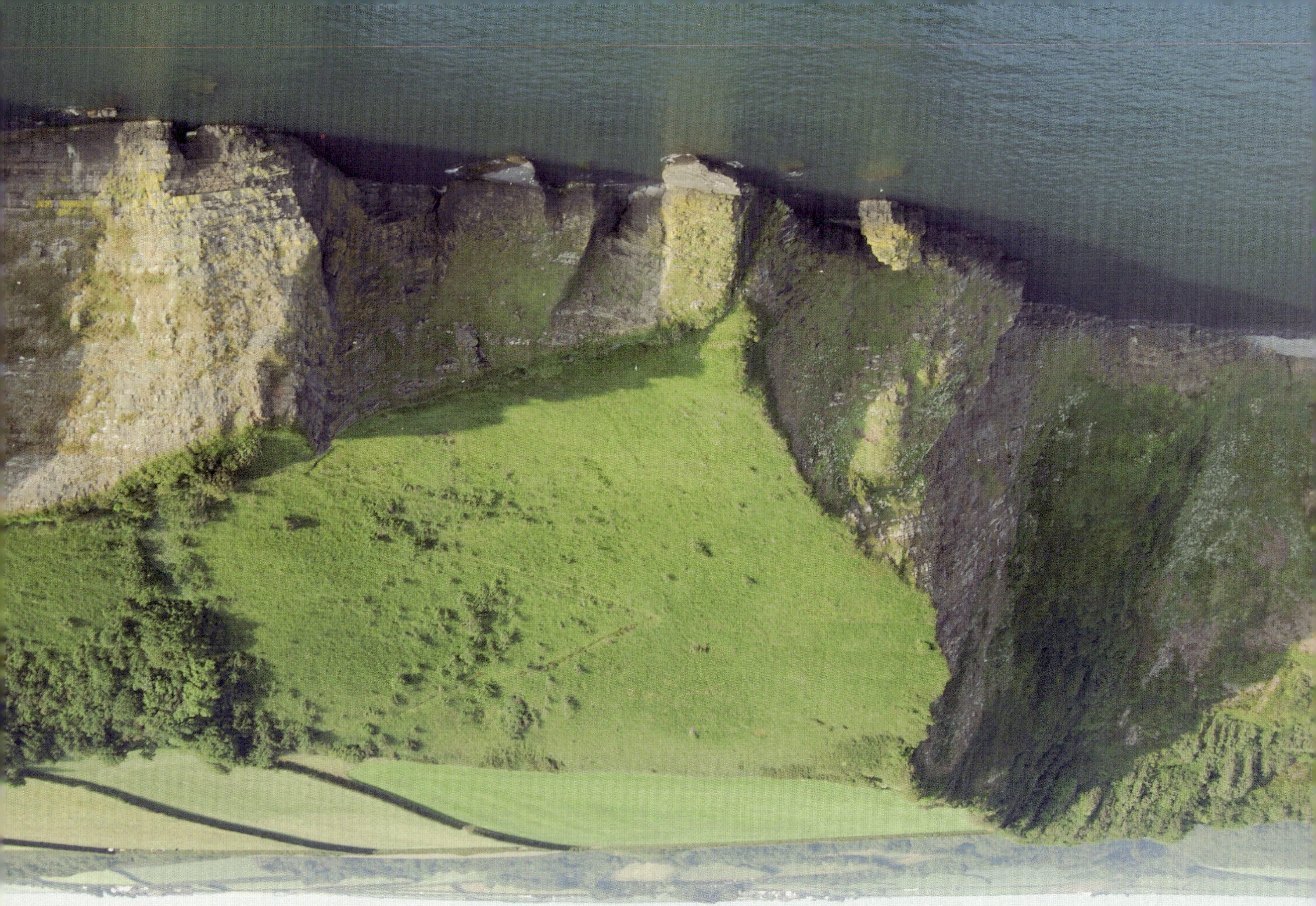

Beckland Cliff. July 1986

On another occasion, I landed at Beckland Beach in rather different weather conditions. I had been following the coast around very close to the shore, wearing no neoprene wet-suit and now set out my soggy wet clothes to dry (right). I decided to light a beach fire to dry myself and clothing. In the shelter of a large boulder I scooped out the shingle to reveal coarse sand. Lit here, the fire will not spit heat-shattered stones. Dead heather from the immediate cliff foot provides kindling. More time than is necessary is spent arranging the kindling into a tiny conical heap, for it is part of the game to light the fire with only one match. I crouch, half Robinson Crusoe, half Peter Pan. One match does it. I then went along the cliff foot to gather a little more timber. At the bottom of a recent scree slope, its foot already winnowed by the sea, I came across this object (below).

Well, I recognised it was a rotary engine and had heard of a World War II bomber crashing into the cliffs hereabouts, so when I was next in Devon I called into Hartland Quay Museum and let them know what I had found. "Oh, look over there in the corner," said the curator. The engine was displayed there with accompanying explanations.

The rotary engine was from a Wellington bomber, part of 172 squadron based at RAF Chivenor and carrying out anti-submarine patrols using powerful searchlights. On 13th April 1942, a Wellington, returning from a training flight in poor visibility, crashed into Beckland Cliffs. All five crew members were killed, one from New Zealand, one from Canada and three from the RAF. A memorial plaque was erected close to the coastal path at the top of Beckland Cliffs in 1988.

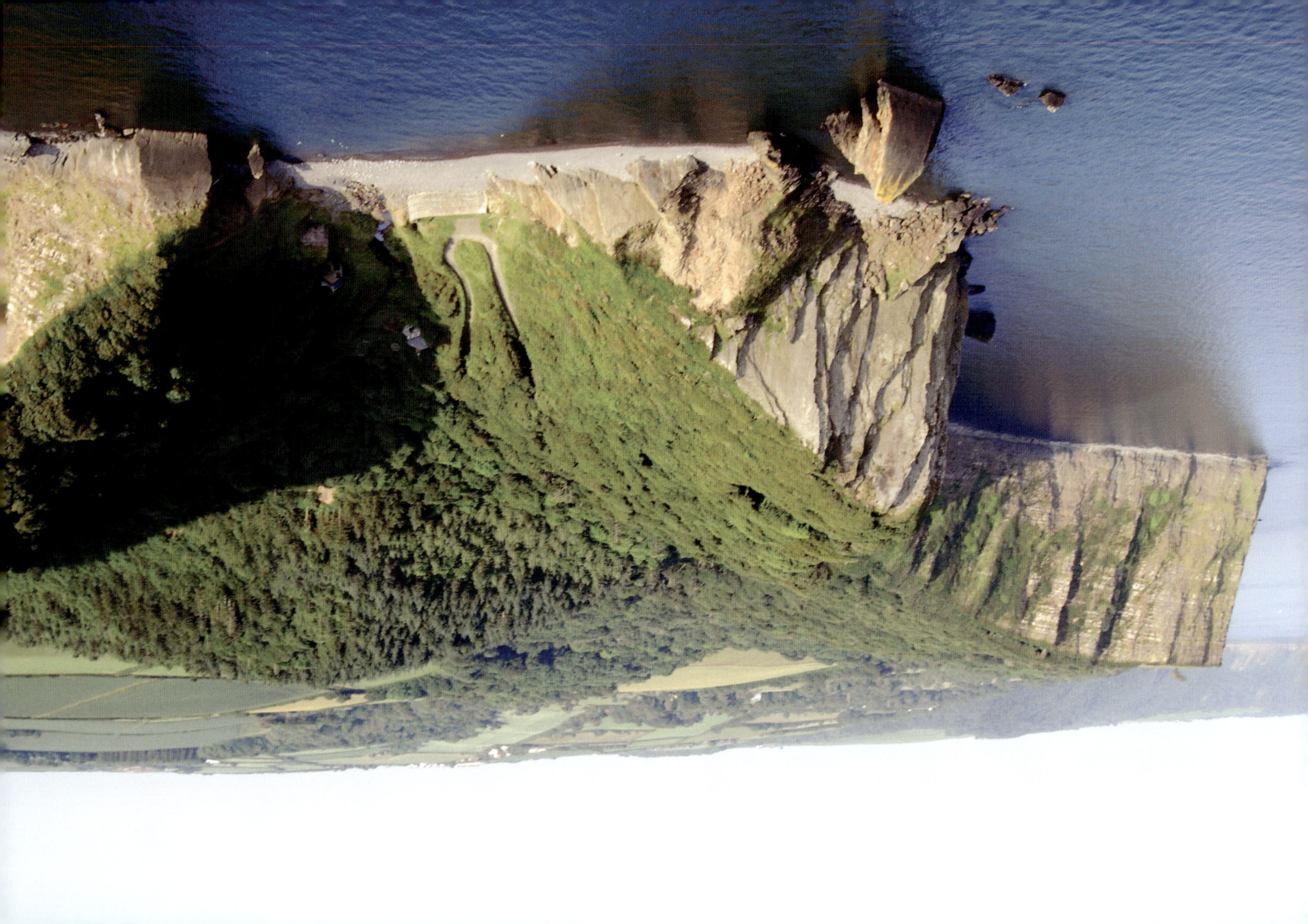

Mouth Mill and Blackchurch Rock

This is one of the more remote beaches which is in fact quite accessible by walking down through the wonderful peace of Brownsham Wood. The Devon Trust for Nature Conservation have even planted a tree library in the wood. Parking is at the National Trust car park at Brownsham Farm at the top of the coombe which leads down to Mouth Mill.

A field exercise? Ways of seeing.

On an introductory field weekend for students taking an integrated Geography Course at Oxford Brookes University, a series of exercises were designed to emphasise the variety of ways in which a landscape could be experienced, some scientific and formal, some not.

My lot was to run an exercise where participants explored the emotional and sensual impact of a place or walk. When I first ran this exercise I thought writing 'poetry' would fill the bill but students were reluctant to expose themselves and those that did tended to write doggerel or rhyming couplets. On the next occasion I suggested a much looser form of writing, a sort of blank verse with words linking description to emotional response which included all the senses. I stressed that this was not an act of communication but something for themselves, capturing something of the emotional impact of the place. In the evening, on an assurance of anonymity I was allowed to collect the 'word paintings'. The results were phenomenal - some condensed almost into Haiku.

My Commonplace Book now has many of my own such jottings, written, I think, for myself. Rereading them they still recapture forgotten experiences. Perhaps you have tried something similar? Anyway, on 30th December 1994, I walked down from Brownsham Farm to Mouth Mill, notebook in hand:

Painting with words: Brownsham to Mouth Mill walk 30th December 1994.

Squelching footsteps gingerly tread mulch of black-dead leaves; focussed wet by the stile.
Search the mud to prove my boots are today's first.
Notice. Devon Bird Trust. "A piece of Devon saved for ever" - Peace of Devon.
In the wood a squall shakes the high branches but the ground green fans of fern are print still.
Dank-still smell of winter wood.
On the right a cross-weave of silver-peeling deciduous branches.
On the left a vertical, tight dark march of conifers.
The trail slides down within the hollow of the valley floor.
A lumbering fist of smashed branches and severed limbs.
Wide-tyred mud; impressions of yesterday's noise.
Extract from words, impressions which press them beyond the tired overused meaning.
Orange gas cylinders lean against the road above the summer cottage.
A limekiln glimpsed through the trees across the stream. Meet no-one.
The stream trenches through the final flat 'head' infill to the beach.
Now the wind tugs. Rain slants my eyes.

A spout of water from the in-spate falls at Windbury Point
arcs, gale-fanned, back over the dead bracken cliff-top.
Toppling failure from land-dipping sandstone sheets, crumble orange onto the grey storm beach.
Black, sea-wet shore-rocks from which plops of white spume suddenly lift and swirl and turn in a flock.
From a dark rock a tern uneasily eyes me from near my feet.
I leave it to die in peace but, lifting with the wind, it glides away.
Struggle to climb the funnelled gale within the arch of Blackchurch Rock
to try photo-framing Windbury waterfalls. The wind pierces my face with slanting hail.
Lie on the rocks to watch boxes of rising giant rollers peak above me on the shore.
Not until I switch to "listen" do they roar and crash against the beach.
Clapotis spouts the sea.
Boulder-jump the stream which gluts brown across the shore to the sea.
Cobbles are polished curved attrition-smooth sandstone; ebony-wet female forms.
Smaller stones have more variety - dark red breccia - flint - obsidian.
Follow the shore towards Windbury, towards a small cave in the black cliff-wall.
I have landed here before; ramping my kayak and springing on-shore before the backwash grips.
Wind-combed trees, black branches cilia-beating against the sky.
Sliding white gannet against black sky - hold my breath - wanna be.
Driven by photography now - exhilarating but angry that it controls.
Momentarily, stand beneath the waterfall but reject the shot, so miss a masterpiece?
Precious solitude but am happy to talk with two visitors entranced by this sea.
Into the smell of the wood again and climb with physical satisfaction, back to the farm.   P.K.

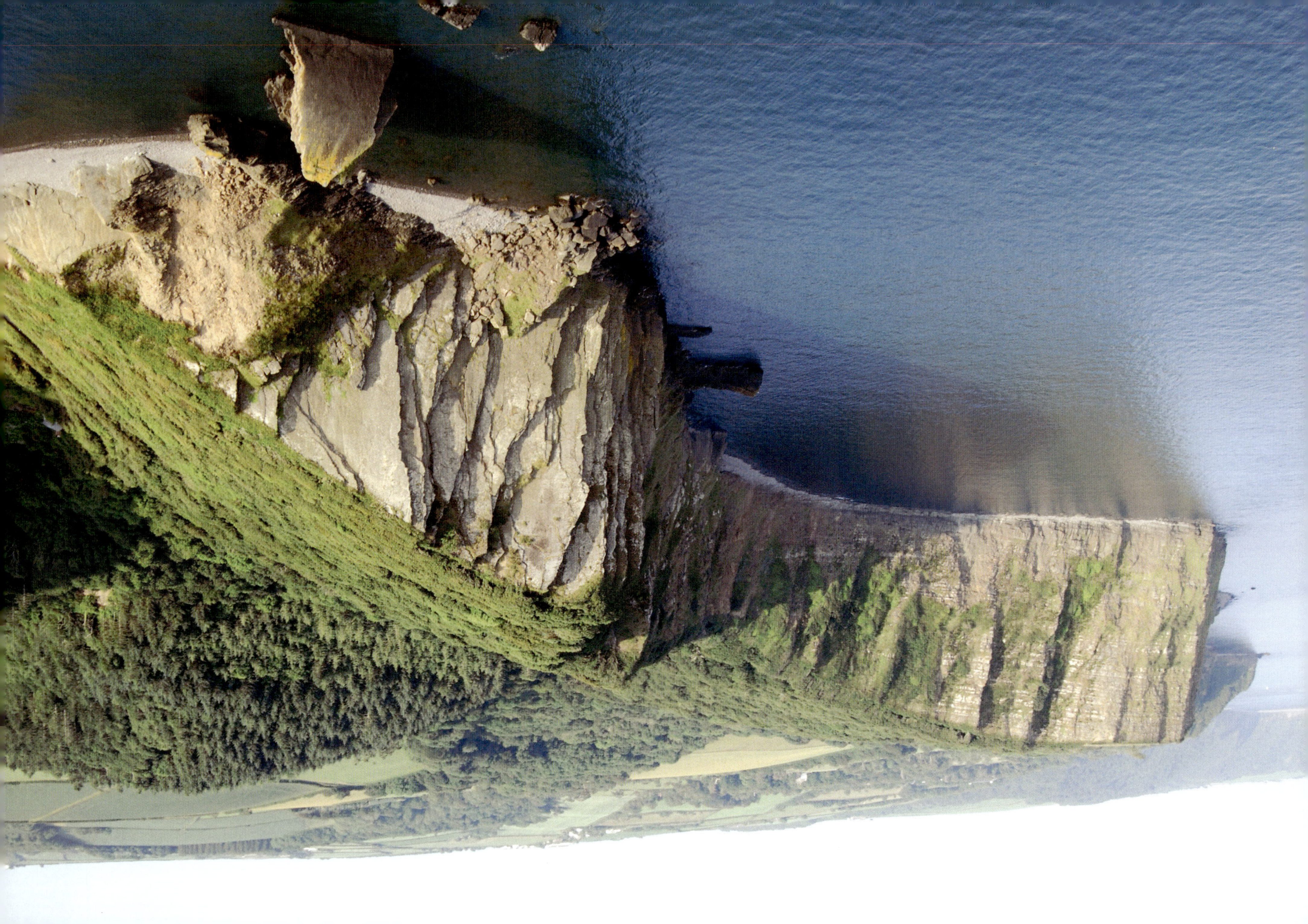

Blackchurch Rock, like Chapman Rock, is a large detached rock mass where the resistant beds of sandstone, dipping seawards, give these rocks a distinctive conical outline, visible for miles along the coast. Within Blackchurch Rock, two sandwiched beds of weaker mudstones have been eroded by the sea producing arches which pass right through the stack.

Above left: Blackchurch Rock viewed from the west
Above right: Etching of Blackchurch Rock in 1822.
Below: Blackchurch Rock viewed from the east with Chapman Rock in the far distance,

My emotional attachment to this coast is by now clear. However, I have, throughout my career had an academic interest in the physical evolution of the local coast, not only in the long term, measured over many thousands of years, but also how the coast has changed in historical times. Before the days of photography, visual information on this was hard to come by but works of art gave some evidence of coastal change, as well as reflecting changing perception of nature and landscape. However, the romantically enhanced 1822 etching (above right), illustrates the pitfalls of examining pre-photography landscape art to evaluate coastal change. It is just possible to kayak through the arch of Blackchurch Rock at high tide but I have good reason to believe, as you may see, that in this case the scale of the etching has been much exaggerated. Can you pick out the image of a fair-sized yacht? However, the etching does indicate that these arches have survived for at least 191 years.

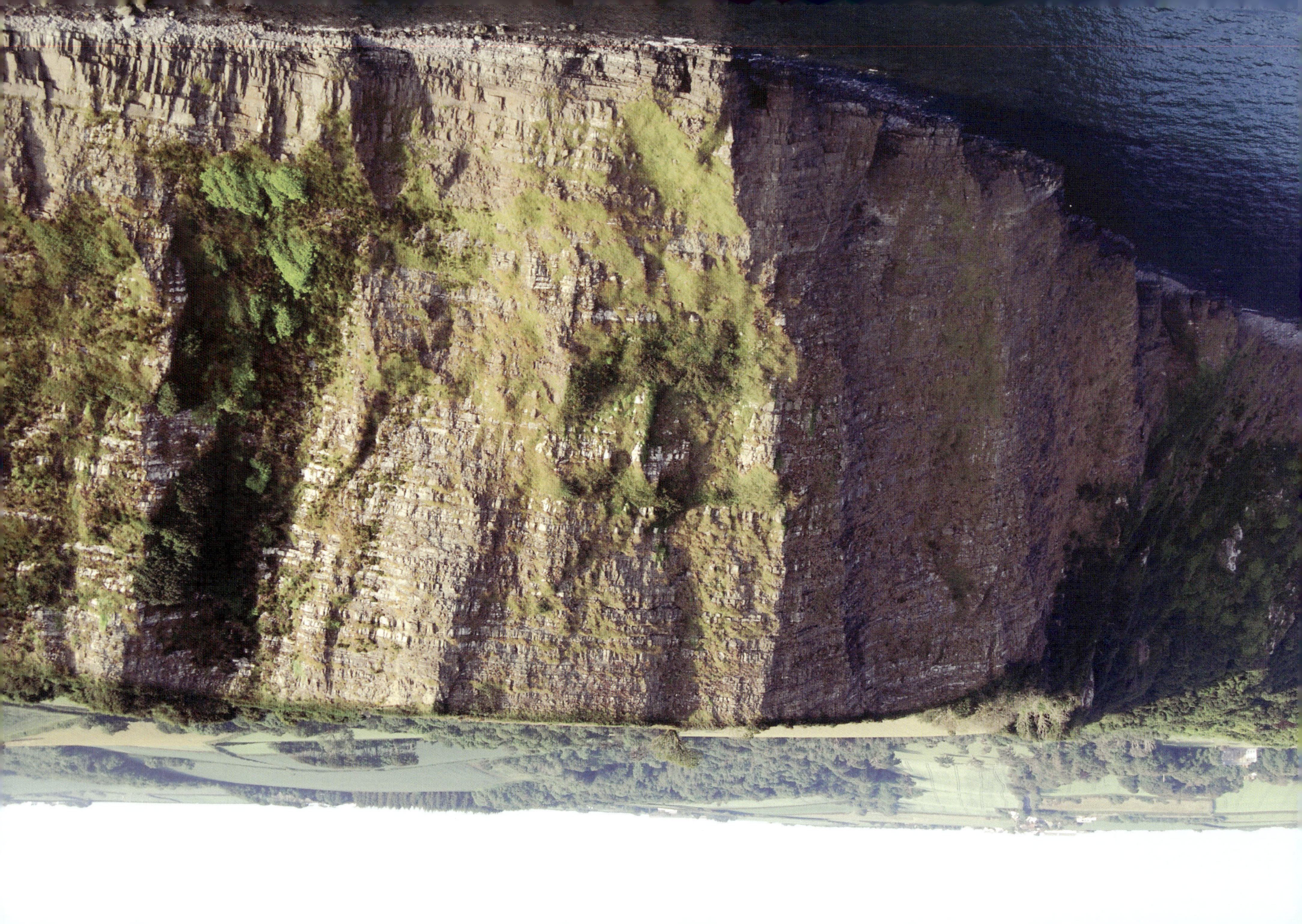

Gallantry Bower. Gallant Cliff. The crest of this precipitous sea cliff of some 400 feet (120 metres) is on the coastal footpath, west out of Clovelly. Near the solitary tree, are the remains of a 3000-year-old burial mound. However, the reward for reaching this hilltop are the panoramic views afforded both along the coast and also simply gazing out from the cliff over Bideford Bay. On the right day you can sit with your picnic for an hour or so just absorbing the changing patterns of clouds over the sea. On a clear day, and with a little imagination, you can just see the tip of the Statute of Liberty, hull down on the horizon, or so I am told!

The direction you may or may not wish to look, is down. But taking care, particularly on a windy day, you can watch seabirds from above. Fulmars, in particular are adept at gliding beneath you without seemingly moving a muscle. Sheer cliffs provide seabirds nest sites with security.

Looking down from a similar high sea-cliff on the Exmoor coast, (Castle Rock in the Valley of Rocks), Southey recorded the following in his Commonplace Book;

"On the summit of the highest point of the hill... I laid myself at length - a level platform of turf spread before me about two yards long, and then the eye fell immediately on the sea - a giddy depth. After closing my eyes a minute, it was deeply impressive to open them on the magnificent dreariness, and the precipice, and the sea."

(Robert Southey 1799)

I had wondered about the use of the words 'magnificent dreariness'. Dreariness perhaps had a slightly different meaning 200 years ago but the closest synonyms I could get that seemed appropriate for the period were melancholy or monotonous.

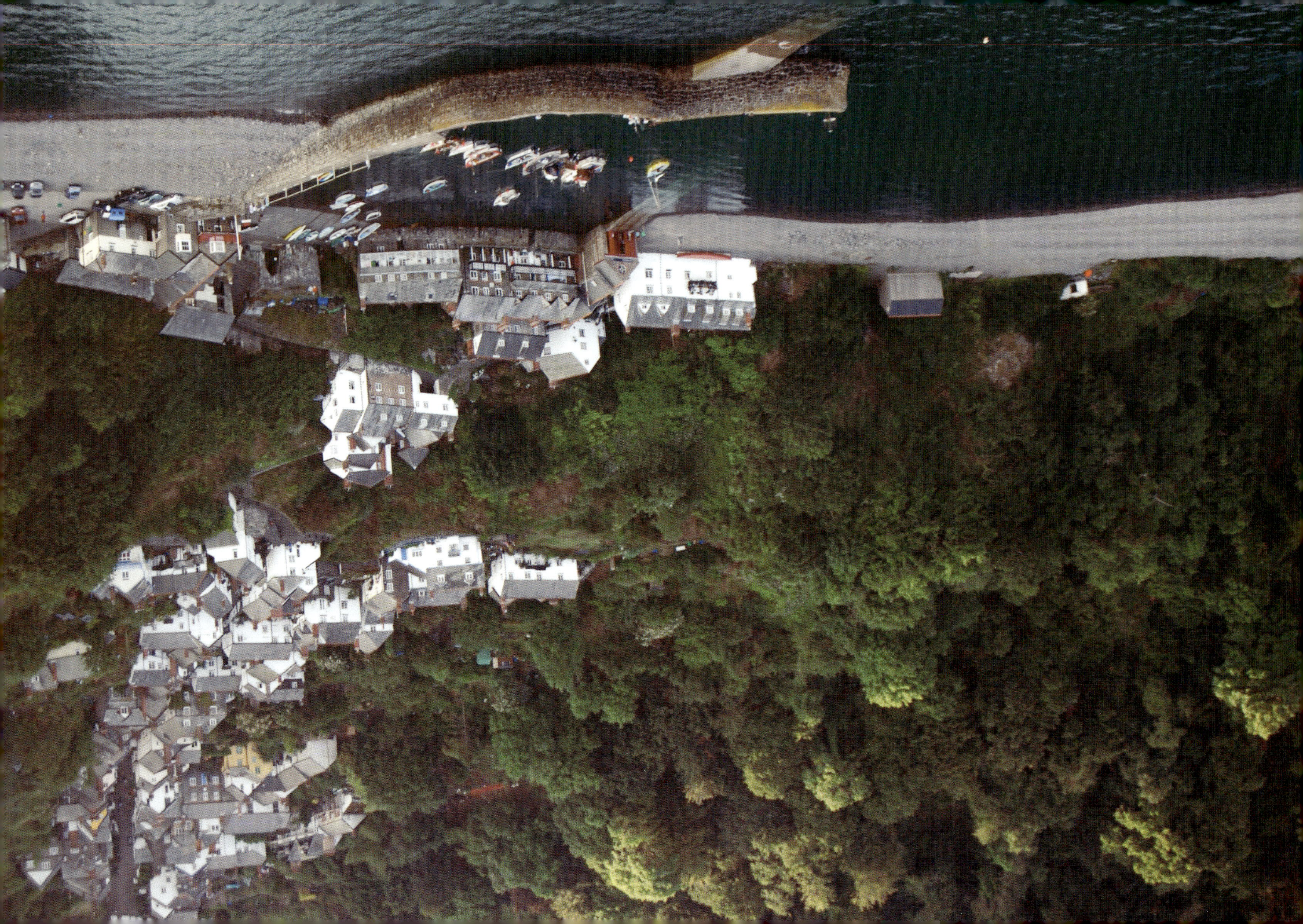

Clovelly

"And a mighty sing'lar and pretty place it is, as ever I saw in all the days of my life!" said Captain Jorgan, looking up at it. Captain Jorgan had to look high to look at it, for the village was built sheer up the face of a steep and lofty cliff. There was no road in it, there was no wheeled vehicle in it, there was not a level yard in it. From the sea-beach to the cliff-top two irregular rows of white houses, placed opposite to one another, and twisting here and there, and there and here, rose, like the sides of a long succession of stages of crooked ladders, and you climbed up the village or climbed down the village by the staves between, some six feet wide or so, and made of sharp irregular stones.

The old pack-saddle, long laid aside in most parts of England as one of the appendages of its infancy, flourished here intact. Strings of pack-horses and pack-donkeys toiled slowly up the staves of the ladders, bearing fish, and coal, and such other cargo as was unshipping at the pier from the dancing fleet of village boats, and from two or three little coasting traders. As the beasts of burden ascended laden, or descended light, they got so lost at intervals in the floating clouds of village smoke, that they seemed to dive down some of the village chimneys, and come to the surface again far off, high above others. No two houses in the village were alike, in chimney, size, shape, door, window, gable, roof-tree, anything. The sides of the ladders were musical with water, running clear and bright. The staves were musical with the clattering feet of the pack-horses and pack-donkeys, and the voices of the fishermen urging them up, mingled with the voices of the fishermen's wives and their many children.

The pier was musical with the wash of the sea, the creaking of capstans and windlasses, and the airy fluttering of little vanes and sails. The rough, sea-bleached boulders of which the pier was made, and the whiter boulders of the shore, were brown with drying nets. The red-brown cliffs, richly wooded to their extremest verge, had their softened and beautiful forms reflected in the bluest water, under the clear North Devonshire sky of a November day without a cloud. The village itself was so steeped in autumnal foliage, from the houses lying on the pier to the topmost round of the topmost ladder, that one might have fancied it was out a bird's-nesting, and was (as indeed it was) a wonderful climber. And mentioning birds, the place was not without some music from them too; for the rook was very busy on the higher levels, and the gull with his flapping wings was fishing in the bay, and the lusty little robin was hopping among the great stone blocks and iron rings of the breakwater, fearless in the faith of his ancestors, and the Children in the Wood."

Clovelly and Charles Kingsley (1819 - 1875)

Before the 1850s Clovelly was a remote, relatively unknown fishing village which, at its peak, harboured over 100 fishing vessels. It is no exaggeration to say that the writings of Charles Kingsley propelled the village into a Victorian tourist destination and in that respect it has never looked back. His father was curate and rector from 1831 to 1836 and Charles Kingsley came to Clovelly in 1831 as a 11-year-old. His village childhood was to have a lasting influence upon him and he drew inspiration from the district throughout his life notably in *The Three Fishers* (1851), *Westward Ho!* (1855), *A Message from the Sea* (1860) and *The Water Babies* (1863).

Charles Kingsley's descriptive introduction (left) to chapter one of *A Message from the Sea* was published over 150 years ago, but still matches with eerie precision today's view which would certainly have been recognised by Kingsley, despite the disappearance of the herring fleet. To read the short story which follows this introduction, download free the full story from Pennsylvania State University Electronic Classics Series.

"Suddenly a hot gleam of sunlight fell upon the white cottages, with their grey steaming roofs and little scraps of garden courtyard, and lighting up the wings of the gorgeous butterflies which fluttered from the woodland down to the garden."
Charles Kingsley

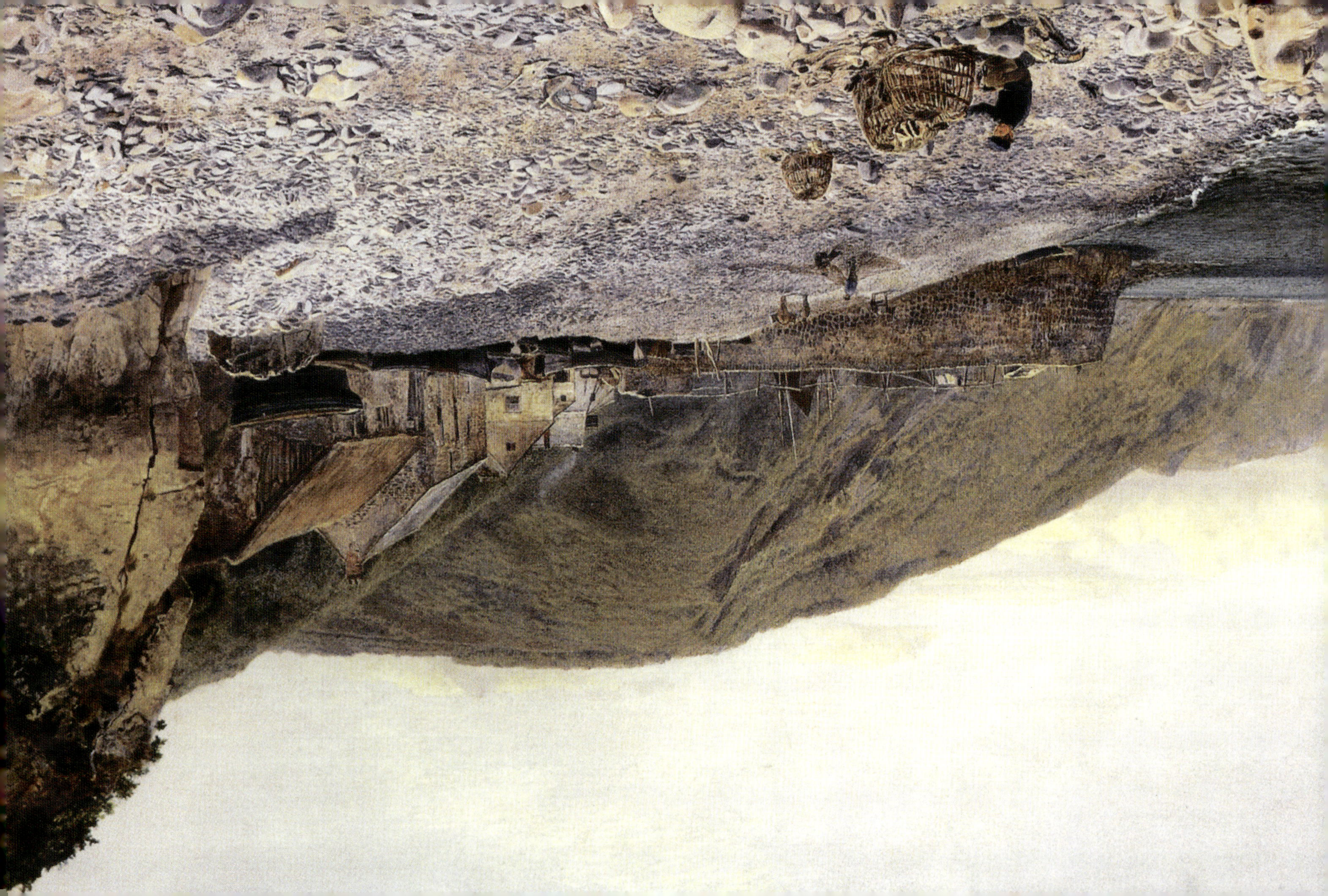

Among the Shingle at Clovelly When visiting the Tate Britain exhibition 'Truth to Nature' in 2004 I was confronted by the above painting, "Among the Shingle at Clovelly" by Charles Napier Hemy (1864). At the time I was looking for old illustrations of this coast to make 'then and now' comparisons. The Blackchurch Rock etching, (page 71) demonstrated one of the problems of using such comparisons but this painting seemed ideal, for Hemy was attracted to the pre-Raphaelite school and its philosophy of 'truth to nature' ensured that their art chronicled as accurately as possible what they saw, down to the last pebble.

To complete my 'then and now' comparision, in 2005 I took a photo (right) from where Hemy had stood and felt hard put to it to recognise any landscape changes. In particular, the rock in the foreground seemed little changed in 140 years, suggesting a sheltered shore with negligible wave erosion, even though the lichen-free pebble storm beach at its foot must be reached by waves during severe storms. The buildings were virtually all identifiable. However, since this photo, the foreshore buildings on the right have been replaced by a new Sail Loft accommodation complex.

When the harbour wall was built, thrusting out into the sea, it created an area (seen here in the foreground) where pebbles collected to form a wide storm beach. Whenever this 'store' becomes full, waves push 'surplus' pebbles around the end of the quay either starting to block the harbour mouth or, eventually, to rejoin the storm beach on the other side of Clovelly. Pebbles over a long period were collected from this beach 'store' to provide building stones and cobbles for the main Clovelly street. Notice how cratered the pebble beach appears in 1864. Recorded in the distance is a donkey loaded with pebbles. Clovelly was expanding and demand for pebbles was high.

At that time it was not recognised that these pebbles were a finite resource and not until 1907 that eminent geologists Newell Arber and Inkermann Rogers confirmed by practical experiment that the pebbles moved continuously from west to east, ultimately being the source of Westward Ho! Pebble Ridge which at that time was diminishing in volume. Proposals in 1911 to limit the removal of pebbles from beaches between Westward Ho! and Hartland to an annual total of between 600 and 1000 tons were unsuccessful and it was many years before a total ban was imposed.

In the early 1950s, during student vacations working in a Bideford High Street beer bottling shop, I would help make deliveries to the Clovelly Red Lion, hard by the harbour wall. The main street being inaccessible to cars, we delivered beer by sledge, sliding down over cobbles, ropes around our shoulders to control the runners over the polished stones. Apart from us, the only beast of burden in the street were donkeys, and we would take an immature delight to bray 'eeyore' to anyone caught in our path. Empty beer bottles, I guess, made their way back to the top of the village by donkey.

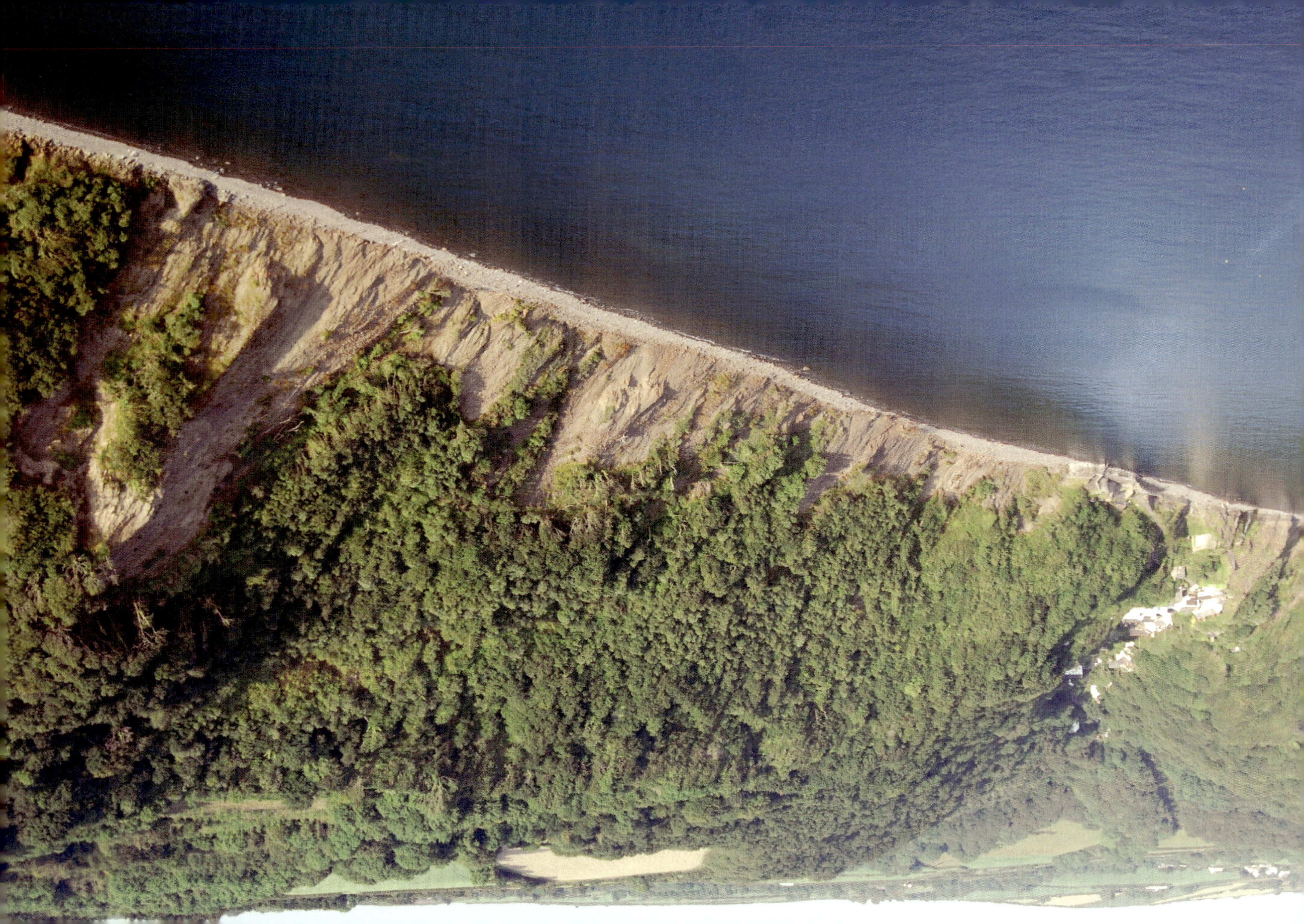

Keivill's Wood From Clovelly to Bucks Mills the coastal slope is clothed with dense green deciduous woods, cliffs only peeping through where small spurs of land have been truncated by the sea. If you are walking the South West Coast Path then the section through the Hobby Drive gives a memorable experience of walking through these woodlands as well as affording spectacular coastal views. This is also a part of a Site of Special Scientific Interest (SSSI), here largely for its woodland and wildlife.

I remember on walks in the mid-1940s from Westward Ho! to Clovelly with my mother and aunt when, if the tide was right, rather than climb up to the main road at Bucks Mills to walk down the Hobby Drive, we would stick to the continuous pebble beach from Green Cliff onwards.

This photo is dated 1946 when I was 10. Pebble hopping on the more stable lower part of the steep storm beach was not too bad but by the Keivill's Wood section and wearing only sandals, I was dead tired.

Hidden by high tide in the photo above, this part of the coast has a remarkable landform, the Gore. This is a 200 metre spit of boulders running out to sea at right angles to the shore. It is thought to be the relic of an ancient unrecorded landslip, first recorded on navigation charts in 1795. All the finer material would have long since have been removed by wave action leaving only the heavier pebbles and boulders as a flat spit.

Above: The Gore at low tide from the air. Here a calm sea sea and clear water reveals The Gore's true extent.
Below: From the coast path above Bucks Mills.

Much of this cliff is unstable as at Keivill's Wood where slips spilling onto the beach have removed swathes of woodland exposing bare earth and rubble. High up on the wooded slope, and today covered in mature woodland, can be seen an old scar which typically forms at the back of such landslips.

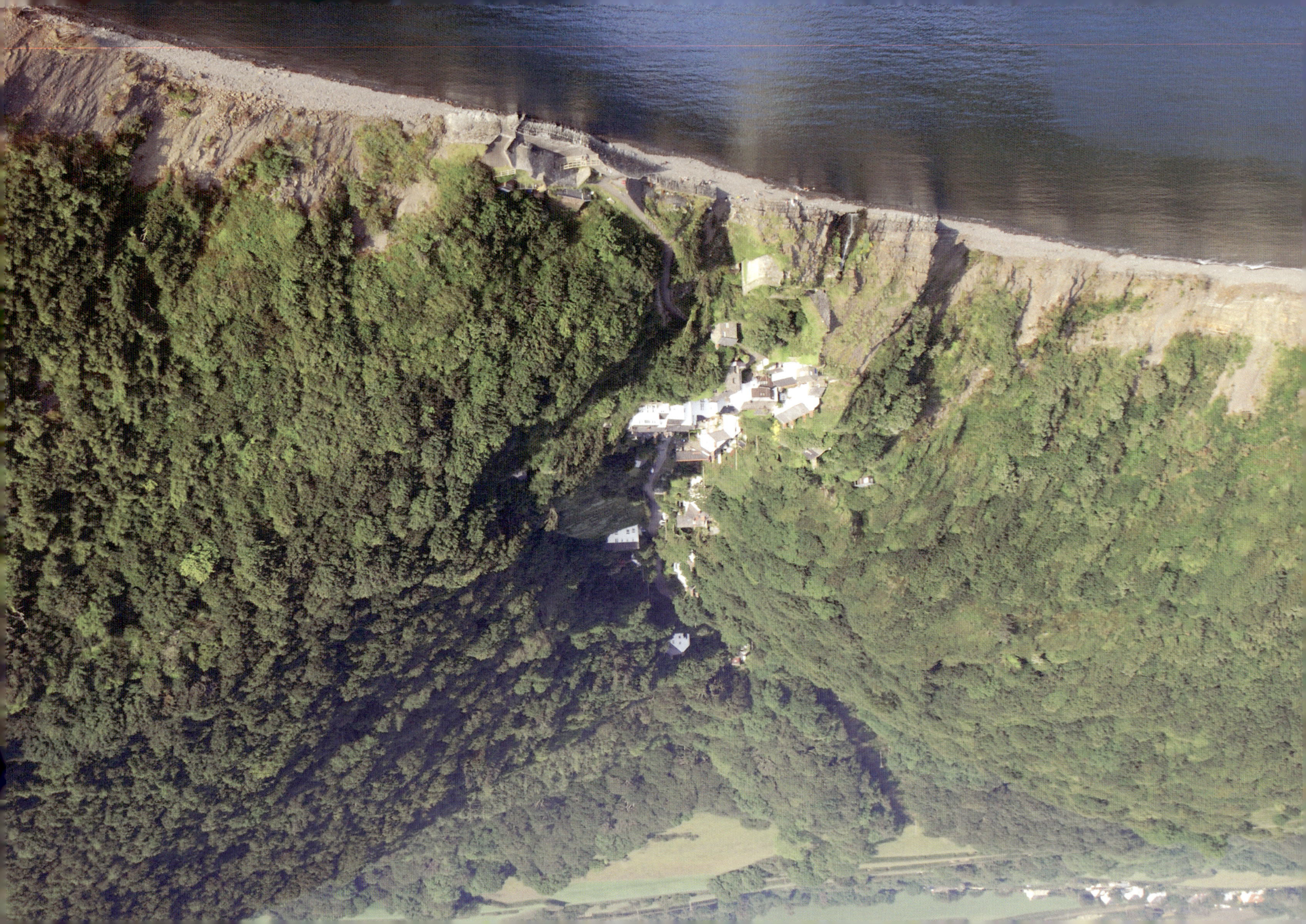

Bucks Mills

Leaving the Atlantic Way (A39) at Bucks Cross, a small road drops towards Bucks Mills, following the floor of a short steep-sided wooded coombe which ends abruptly, hanging above the beach. The stream which had followed the floor of the coombe here pours over the cliff edge in a cascade and waterfall which plunges directly onto the beach (see photo above). In spate this waterfall is very impressive. The village itself shares the narrow valley floor with the stream, buildings being scattered on either side of the single street which also ends, perched above the sea. At the seaward end of the village several building seem destined to tumble to the beach in the foreseeable future, a function of the sea erosion which is readily apparent on most stretches of this coast. Visitors must park at the top of the village. There then follows a pleasant walk down through the village and, where the street ends, a steep track, hinted at in the Turner etching (below), leads down to the shore. In March 1989, much of this track, linking the village with the shore, was swept away by a landslip and rock falls blocked access to the shore. No organisation would take responsibility for any repair and for some time it appeared that the track would never be reinstated. In fact it was not until 1993 that, after gabion cages stabilised the landslip that the route was reopened. The 2009 air view seems to show that the hillside above the track is stable enough to be covered in thick vegetation. However, the toilets built by the hard to serve the beach were never reinstated, the track being considered not strong enough to take the weight of the lorries needed to service the toilet facilities.

Painting and Landscape

"In the nineteenth century, paintings of local scenes and of fishing folk did much to popularise the sea coast away from the by now well-established resorts for sea bathing all round the coast of England. An early visitor to Bucks Mills (1824) was JMW Turner who, [from a spot close to the top of the steep path which descends to the beach] painted a watercolour, 'Clovelly Bay'. This was quickly turned into an accurate etching by William Miller (Turner's favourite engraver) and published in 1826 as part of a series entitled 'Picturesque Views of the Southern Coast of England'.

The sweeping view [right] includes distant Lundy, Gallantry Bower, Blackchurch Rock, Clovelly and, in the foreground, one of the Bucks Mills limekilns. In the middle distance is the Gore, here providing some shelter and a pebble bank upon which small vessels can be beached."
(John Bradbeer,
'Bucks Mills, people and place' 2011)

5

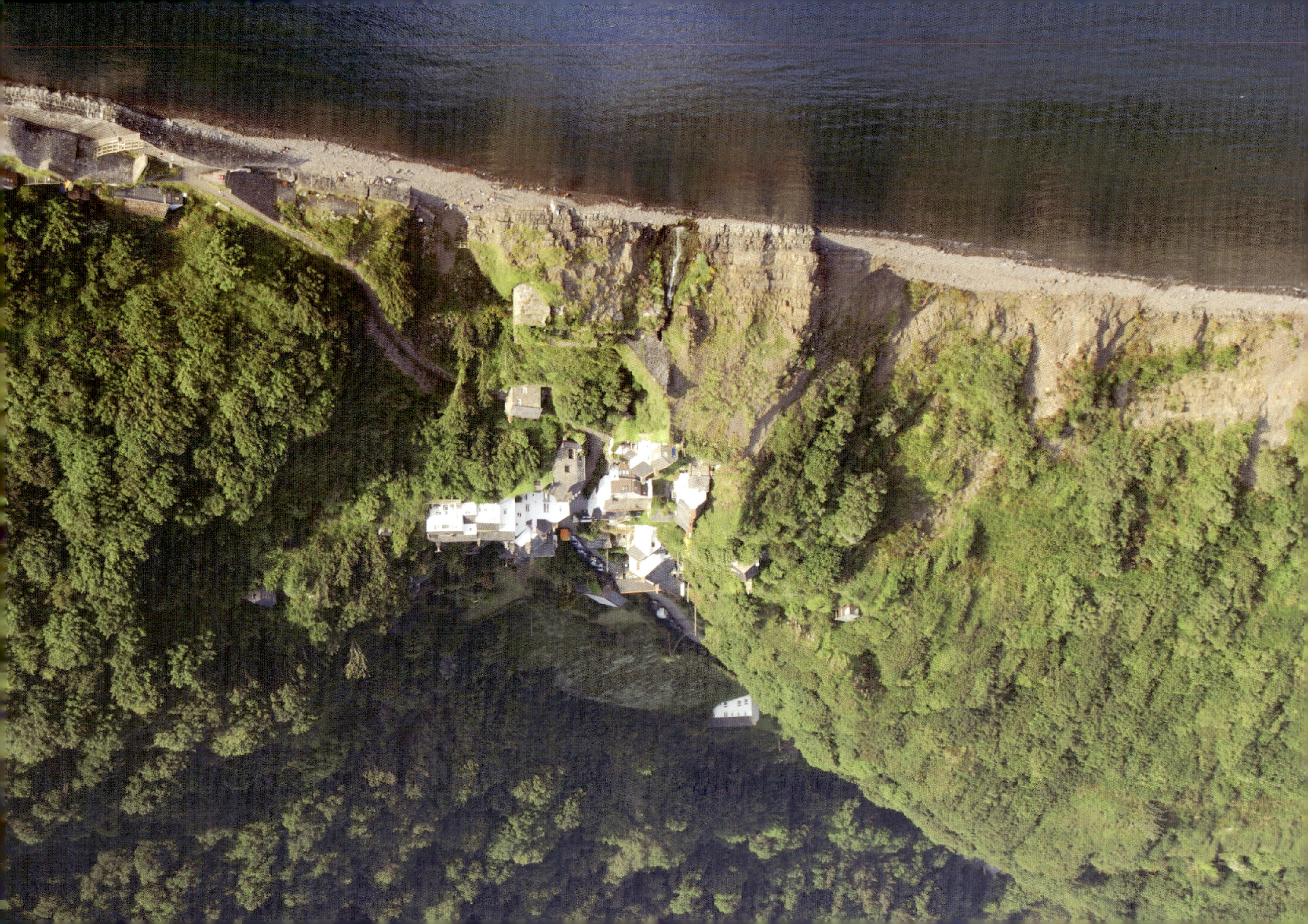

The Lucy at Bucks Mills (right), painted in 1990 by Michael Lees, recreates the tradition of 'beach work' well-established on the coast of North Devon by the end of the sixteenth century.

Beach work. Wherever there was no nearby sheltered haven to unload bulky goods such as coal, timber and limestone, when weather conditions allowed, small sailing vessels would run aground at high tide onto a convenient beach, unload or load their cargo and, with luck, depart on the next tide. Even where there were quays, such as at Hartland, beach work was the norm. For sailing vessels this operation demanded great skill and experience.

The prevalence of ruined limekilns all along the North Devon coast demonstrates the importance of the trade until the late nineteenth century when improved rail and road transport and the growing use of artificial fertilisers sent the trade into steep decline.

The Limekilns. *"There are two limekilns at the beach. ... The western kiln ... is typical of the many limekilns all round the North Devon coast. Lime and coal were put into the kiln through the firing hole at ground level and the draught hole was at the top of the kiln. The kiln was charged and the lime burnt and allowed to cool before being dug out. The lime was usually slaked in water before being carted away for use on the fields. The basic structure is much better seen at Clovelly, as the kiln on the harbour side there can be viewed from above when descending from the cobbled High Street.*

The large eastern kiln is often mistaken for a castle and was of a different design to the western kiln. It had an inclined plane or ramp running down to the top of the kiln so that it could be recharged with coal and limestone whilst still alight. The inclined plane has suffered from passing years and no longer reaches the kiln top. The eastern kiln was constructed about 1760. Lime burning was a hazardous business, with the temperatures needed to reduce the limestone being high and the resulting material highly caustic.

For much of the nineteenth century, the trade in lime and the limekilns on the beach were a principal activity in Bucks Mills. Lime was in demand as a building material but especially for agricultural purposes. North Devon's soils are almost everywhere acid and particularly so on the Culm Measures in the hinterland of Bucks Mills. Perhaps as early as the sixteenth century, the practice arose of importing limestone, burning it to yield quick-lime, then dousing this in water to produce slaked-lime and spreading this on the land. The practice became particularly widespread during the eighteenth century when agricultural methods were modernised and particularly where local landlords were keen to be seen as "Improving Land-Owners". Most of the littoral land-owning families had at least one limekiln on their property by the mid-nineteenth century. For most of North Devon, both the limestone and coal had to be imported from South Wales. Pembrokeshire coal fields, rather than those in Glamorgan were the principal source of coal for North Devon's limekilns."

John Bradbeer. (2011) *'Bucks Mills, people and place'*

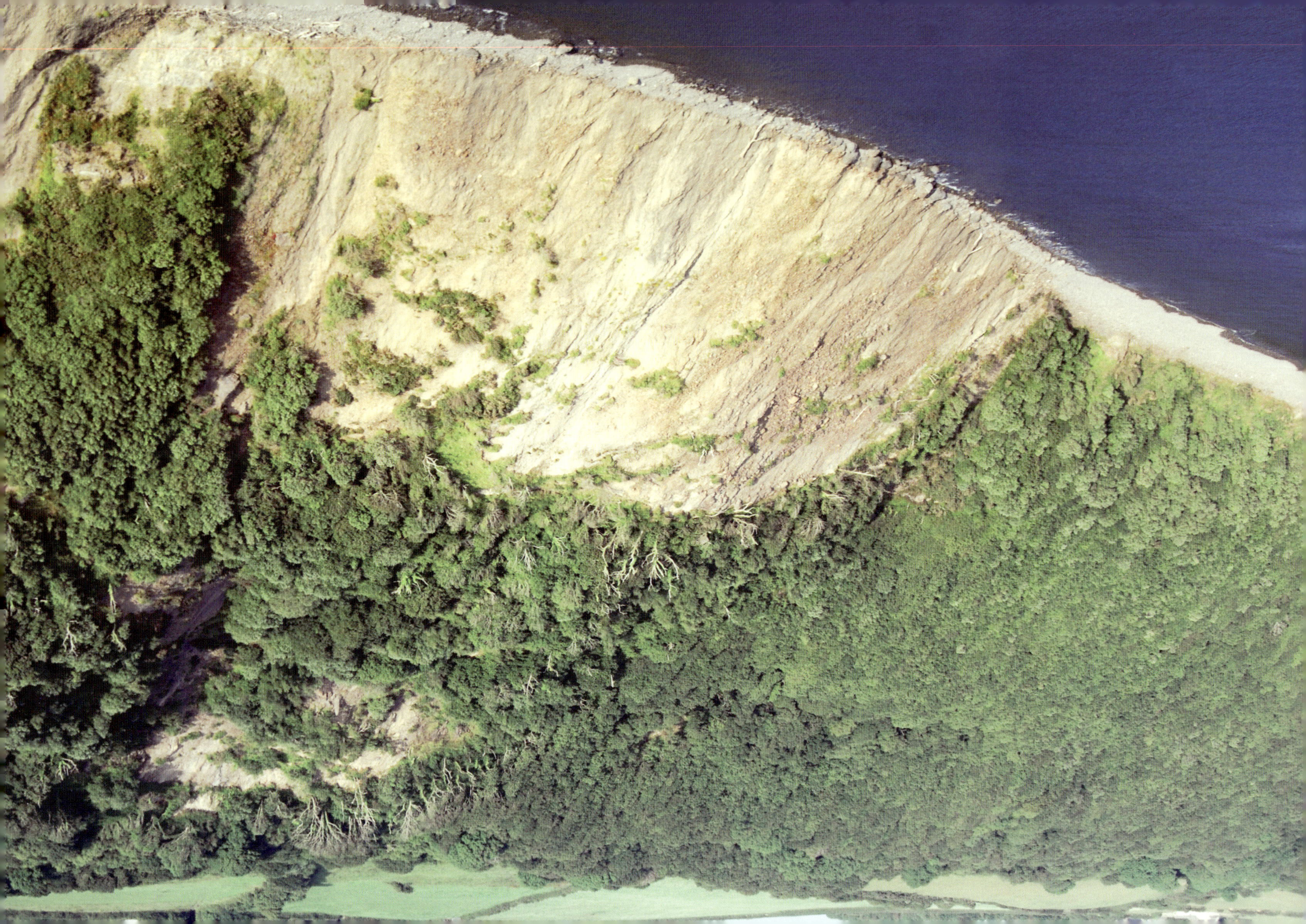

Worthygate Wood

To the east of Bucks Mills the densely wooded hillside touches the beach and cliffs are absent but the view is dominated by a very active landslip. Near the top of the wooded area the curved scar marks where this cliff failure began. As the mass of the landslip moved down slope it rafted a block of living woodland but this is being overcome by the chaotic mass movement of earth and debris until, towards the beach, the bare bulging toe of the slip is spilling onto the beach. On the positive side, in time this debris will be integrated into the beach which generally provides protection against wave attack eroding the shore. Intervention will usually depend upon the value of the land under threat.

Beneath wooded cliffs, kayaking in the sheltered shore of the **Bight a Doubleyou** makes for an easy passage close to the beach, enabling one to enjoy the cliffs and birds. Exposed between the tides are great spreads of large, dark angular blocks of stone, the long forgotten remnants of old cliff falls and landslips. In time these will be reduced to rounded pebbles and will join the grey storm beach in its wave-driven march towards Westward Ho! As one moves east around the bay the shore gradually becomes more and more exposed.

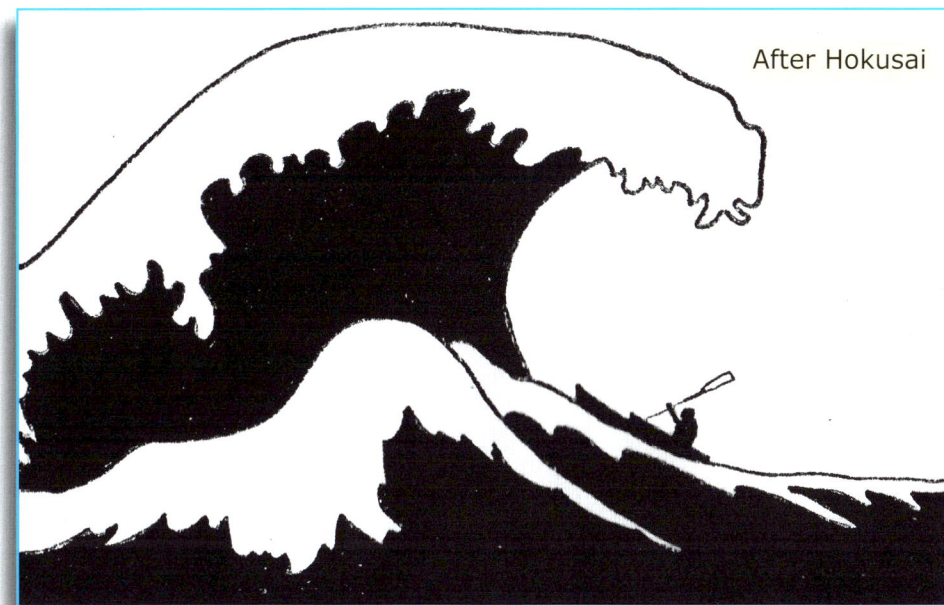

After Hokusai

Describing the joy of kayaking this coast would not be complete without mentioning my friends the seals. I have no anthropomorphic illusions about our contact but I seldom spent a day on the sea hereabouts without my solitude being broken by the inspection of an inquisitive seal. Perhaps because the passage of a kayak is so silent, a seal would sometimes surface very close by and then, after a sharp snort, immediately dive as if taken by surprise. However, at other times we would simply silently stare at each other for some minutes before, closing its nostrils it slowly sank, sometimes visibly rolling beneath the kayak to surface again to examine me from a different angle. What it thought of me I know not but for me it was a pleasant communion. I never did get a decent photo locally of these meetings but kayaking with friends in Scotland I took this shot which sums up our encounters.

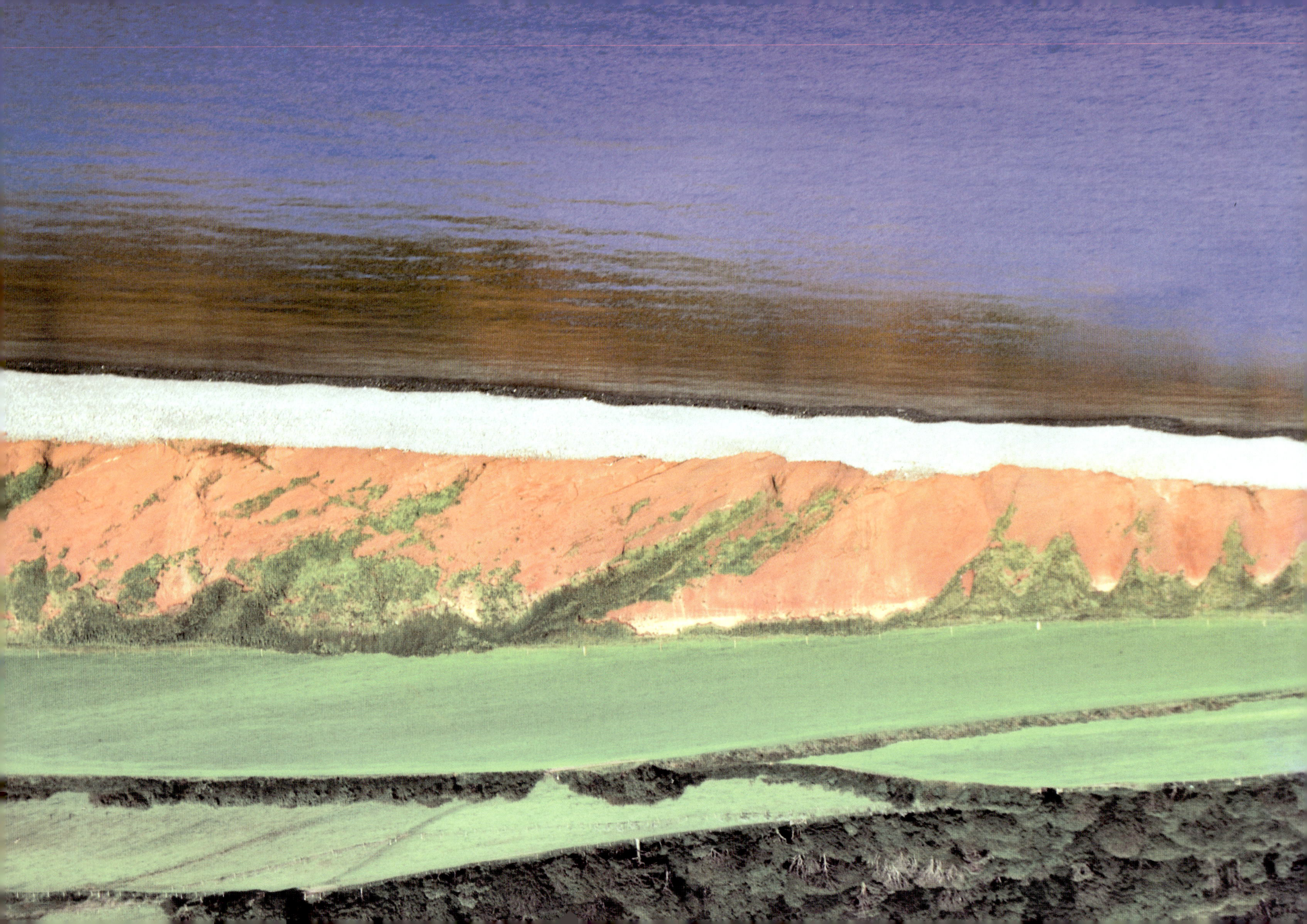

Peppercombe - Portledge Cliffs From the sea these cliffs are a sharp splash of colour when compared with the sombre Carboniferous rocks of the rest of this coast. Landing from my kayak I often start dreaming in my time-travelling mode, imagining myself in the environment where each rock was formed. Sitting at the bottom of a Carboniferous sea is not too exciting but in this red Permo-Triassic environment it offers a bit more scope. Some 220 million years ago I find myself in an arid environment, something like the Sahara, surrounded by sand, stained red by oxidation commonly found in desert conditions. I am standing in a wadi, the steep walls of which are clothed in screes of rock fragments, later to be cemented together by white calcite to form a breccia or, where the fragments are rounded, a conglomerate. The floor of the wadi is coated with fine red sediments deposited from the last flash flood.

It is thought that, at one time, these red sandstones covered a much larger area in North Devon but were eroded, and today, are only preserved here in a deep trough caused by faulting.

On the storm beach I found a wave-rounded sandstone pebble (see below) which tells its story of these rocks rather nicely. I strap the pebble to my flat rear deck, normally reserved for seals, and made my way homewards. Today that rock sits in my study and, like my Commonplace word painting, reminds me vividly of past pleasures.

The grey pebbles of the storm beach are simply travelling through, imported from the right and exiting stage left. Local red pebbles, derived from these cliffs are common enough on this beach, but seldom survive long travelling east in the violent wave-driven conveyer belt of pebbles.

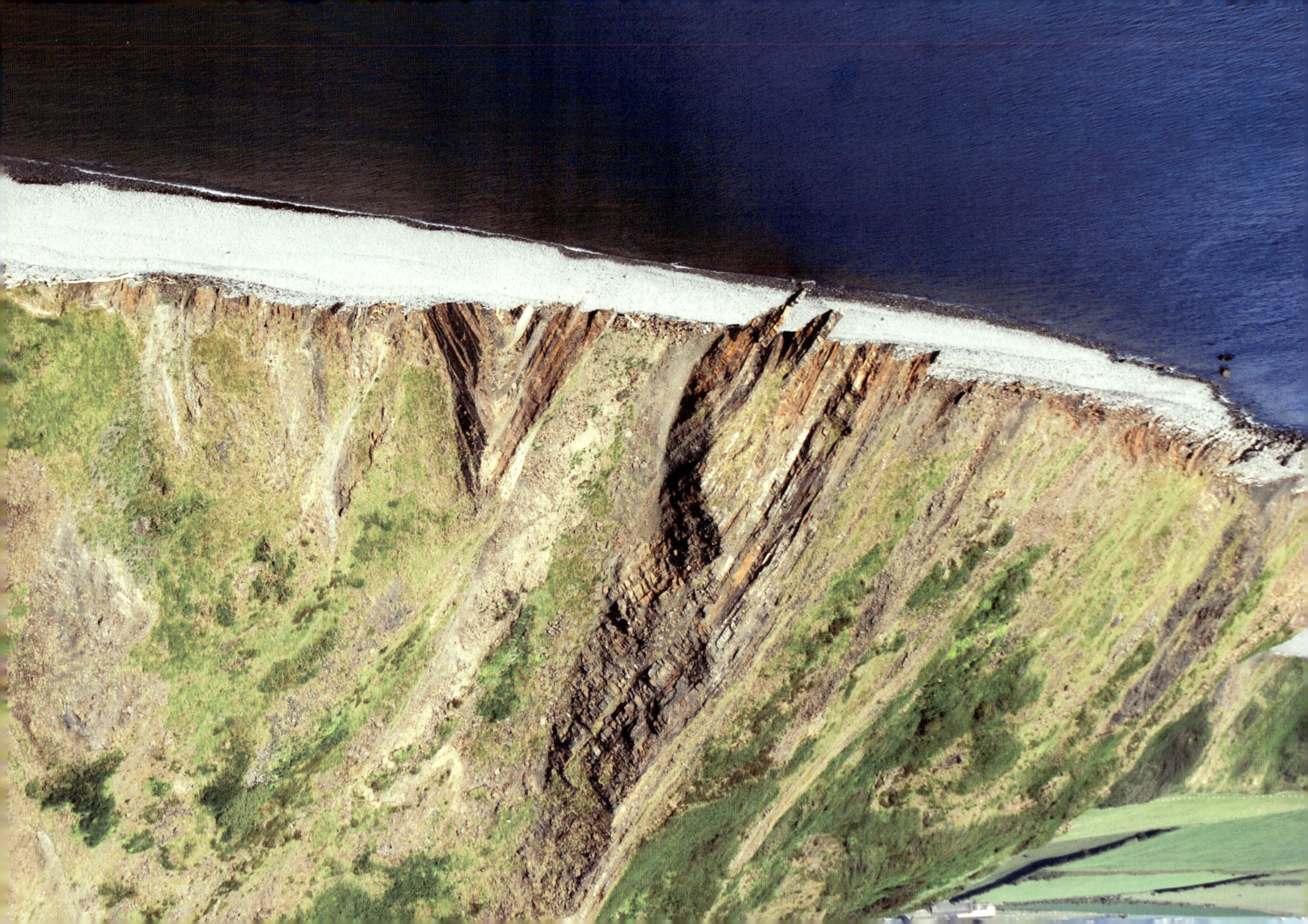

Cockington

The very sharply folded rock beds at the base of Cockington Cliff are known as Tut's Hole (I don't know the origin of the name) which is a striking feature of this shore. In fact, seeing it from the air in 2009 was not at all as I remembered it. Looking back through my records it proved to be yet another reminder that even the hardest rocks, of such a coast as this, are constantly retreating under attack by waves and weather.

Tut's Hole

Above: Geologist Newell Arber visited this coast with his photographer before publishing his book in 1911. He notes;

"The great feature of interest here is the very fine anticline known as Tut's Hole. This is a sharp fold of a series of sandstone beds, some of which are four feet in thickness, projecting clear from the cliff. The anticline has become broken at its crest, and the sides are beginning to crumble away. In 1903, it measured fifty feet in height and seventy feet across the base." [Newell Arber offers himself for scale]

Top right: 1960. My first Geography field week at Westminster City School under the watchful eye of my Head of Department. Rigorous walks were the order of the day, punctuated by mini-lectures in front of features of interest including here at Tut's Hole.
Bottom Right: Tut's Hole circa 1963. A tea stop during a kayak trip.

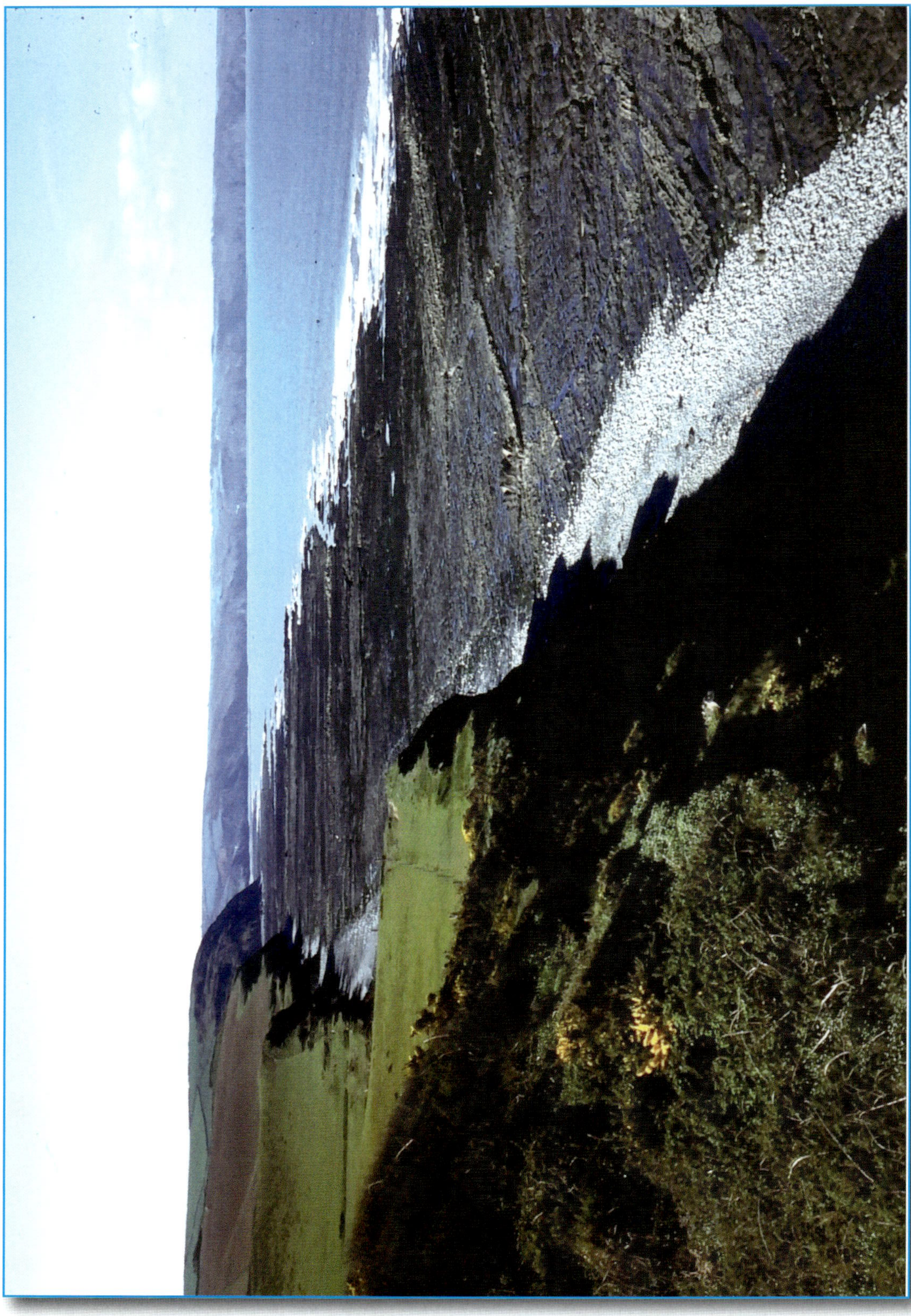

Above: **Cornborough looking west**   The great rounded hog's back cliff, dark with gorse and undergrowth rising in the middle distance is Cockington. The coast has now swung around to face the north-east with a wide rocky shore exposed at low tide with beds trending seawards again but on this stretch with few prominent reefs. The South West Coast path takes you along these cliff tops. From the crest of Cockington the view over the low tide rocky shore platform is superb. I look at the rocks below with wonder. Is it that I have some sense of the forces and the timescale required to produced this view or is it really a question of letting the landscape speak? Pass.

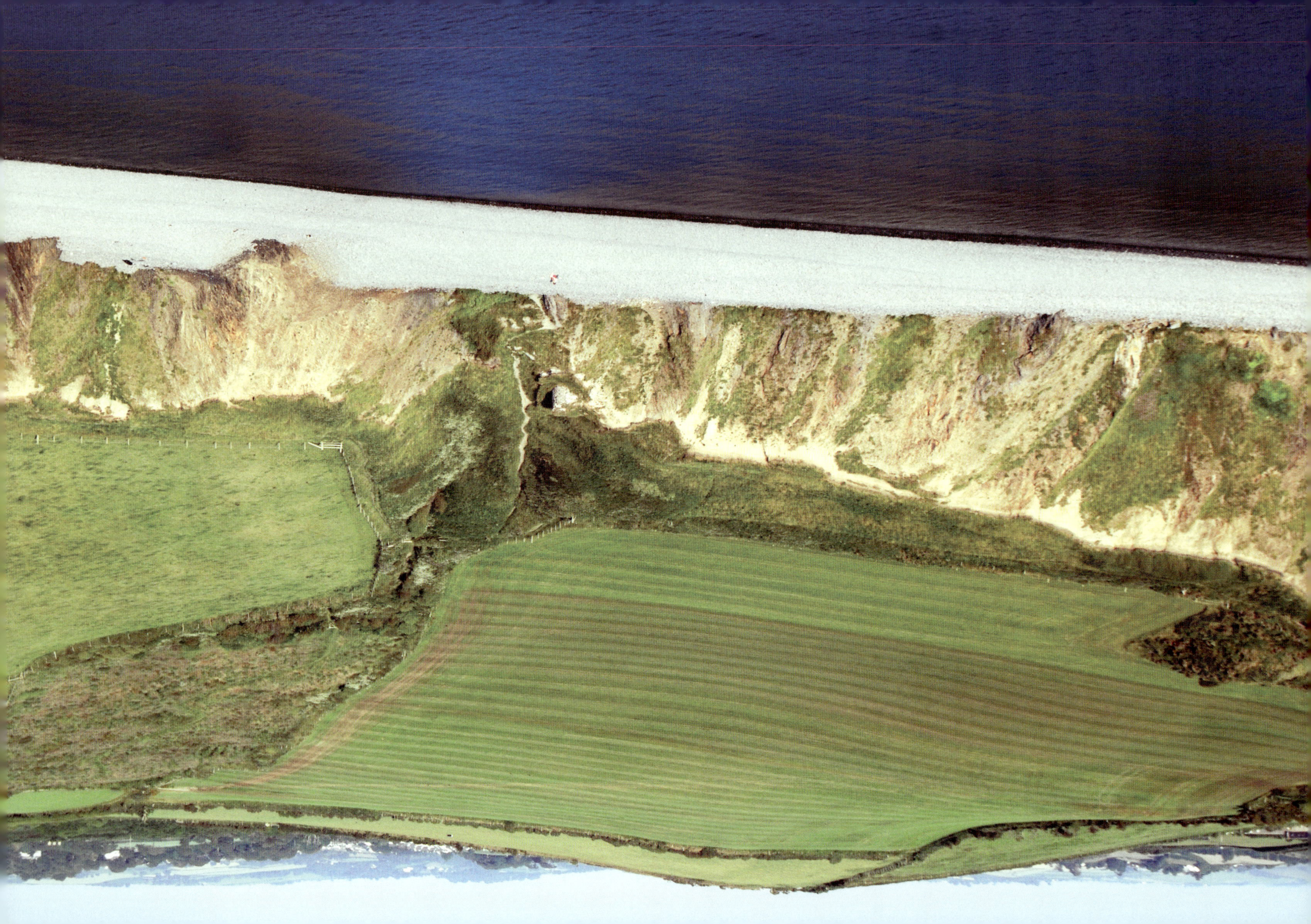

Green Cliff

This small coombe at Green Cliff allows a track access to the shore and provided the incentive to build a small limekiln where the coombe met the sea.

Newell Arber notes that the seam of anthracite which outcrops just to the east of the coombe (see the disturbed ground on the extreme left of the air photo above) was working in 1805. Small fragments of anthracite in the vicinity of the kiln lends credence to reports that this was used in the kiln although most of the fuel probably arrived by sea. The 'coal' seam is still visible where the seam (some two feet thick) meets the shore, immediately below the workings above. Landslips obscure this

Left: A field lecture to a captive audience of Geography pupils from Westminster City School in 1960. I told them about limekilns and beach work. I didn't realise at the time it was something I was to do frequently over the next 40 years! We marvelled at the way the softer sandstones in the kiln wall had weathered and also uncovered layers of limpet shells (modern kitchen midden) presumably being the remains of snacks gathered on the sea shore by kiln workers in the nineteenth century. I later tried this delicacy but found them as tough as old boots.

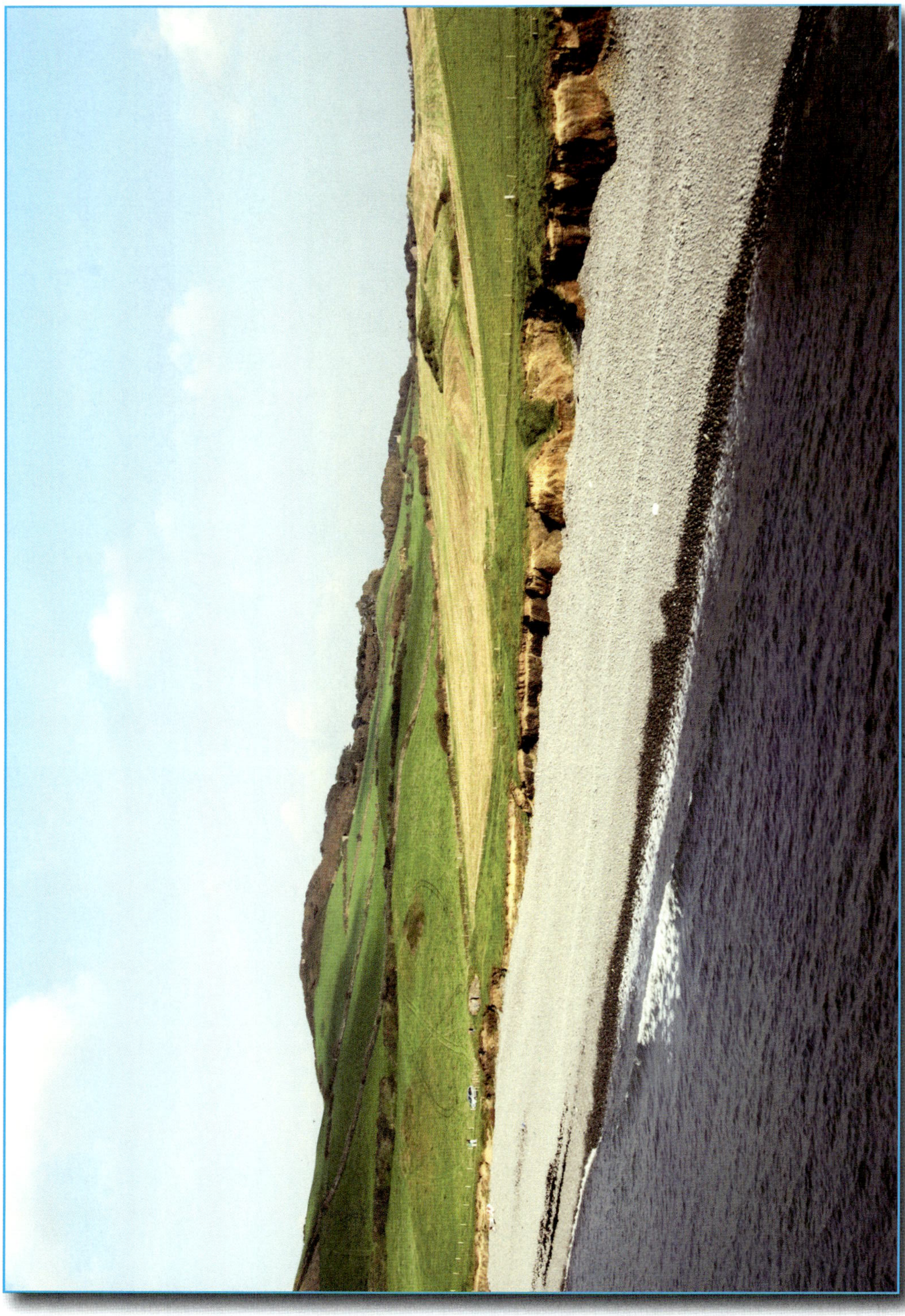

In April 1981 walking the coast path towards Cockington with my son, we came across this wreck. Stephen briefly took command!
By September 1983 all that remained were rusting shattered plates.

Cornborough. As well as boasting at one time or another, a race course, a rifle range and the inevitable limekiln, this lowland trough proved a convenient route for a railway to reach the coast from Bideford before turning east through cliff cuttings to Westward Ho! and, eventually, Appledore. The railway was opened in 1901. The postcard (below left) shows the train on Bideford Quay. The postmark looks like August 1911. The one unpunctuated sentence message reads: *"This is the train we went to Westward Ho! yesterday a very grand place and plenty of sea and bathing tents very funny is it not the train runs on the road and we are having grand weather much enjoying ourselves"*. The 2nd card postmarked 1904 shows the train puffing up the Kenwith valley towards Cornborough. The railway was dismantled in 1917, yet on an early morning walk through the cliff cutting between Westward Ho! and Cornborough a ghost of the railway track emerged, painted in frost.

6

A truculent Cornborough resident 1960. A North Devon Red.

From above Cockington looking north-east along the coast at low tide. The grey storm beach snakes along the cliff foot passing Green Cliff, Cornborogh and Rock Nose, beyond which it swings east towards a hidden Westward Ho! White breakers mark the seaward edge of the great lowlands sweep of the Taw-Torridge Estuary. Beyond that lies the upland mass of Exmoor.

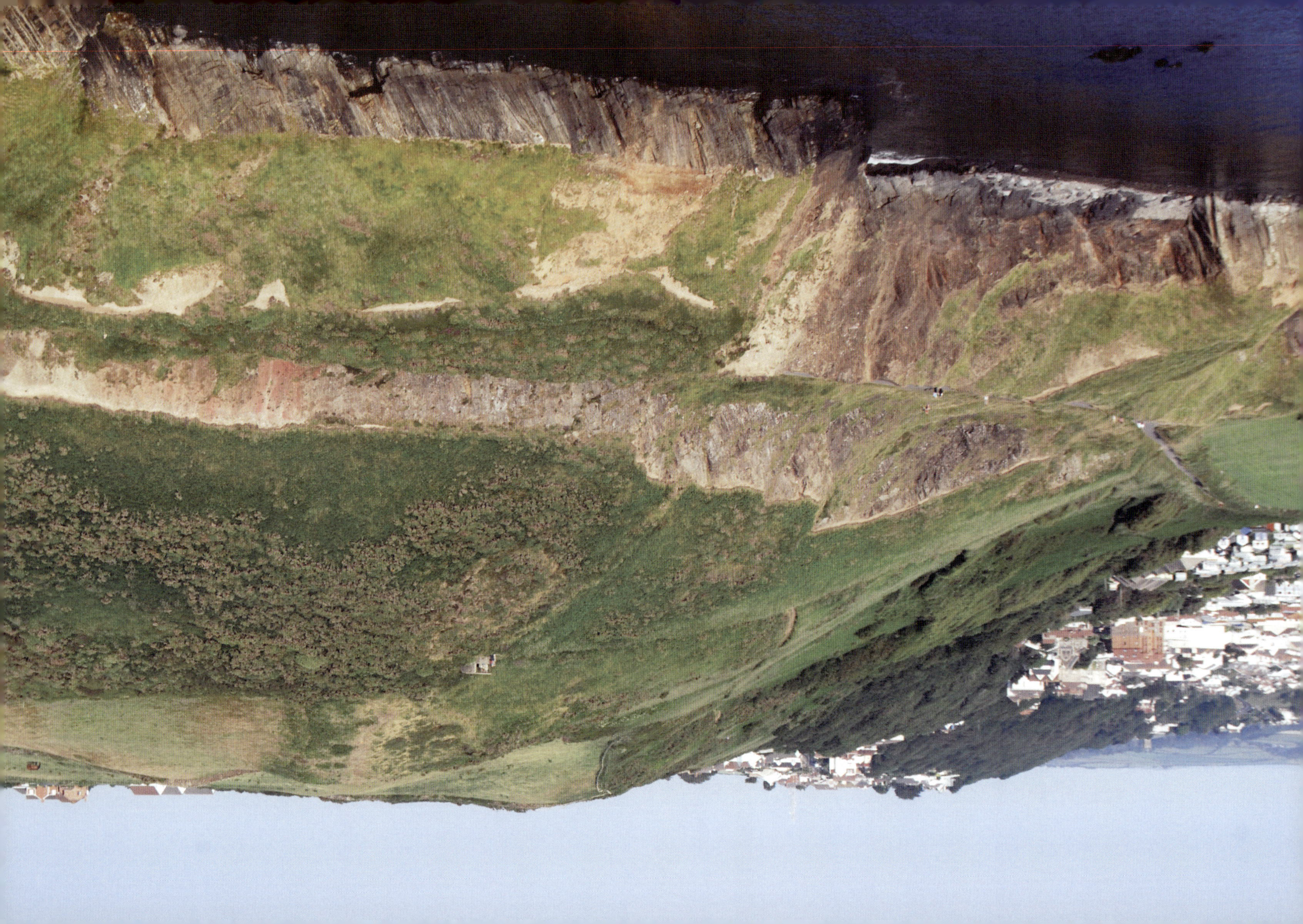

Kipling Tors (Furze Hill), Westward Ho!

Cliff-top prospect Rudyard Kipling and his adolescent college friends from the United Services College, Westward Ho! find a remote hideaway amongst the gorse (furze), probably located near the western end of the cutting shown in the air photo, although, of course the railway cutting didn't exist at that time.

> "Down that tunnel [through the gorse] they crawled. It was evidently a highway for the inhabitants [foxes] of the combe; and, to their inexpressible joy, ended, at the very edge of the cliff, in a few square feet of dry turf walled and roofed with impenetrable gorse.
>
> 'By gum! There isn't a single thing to do except lie down,' said Stalky, returning a knife to his pocket. 'Look here!'
>
> He parted the tough stems before him, and it was as a window opened on a far view of Lundy, and the deep sea sluggishly nosing the pebbles a couple of hundred feet below. They could hear young jackdaws squawking on the ledges, the hiss and jabber of a nest of hawks somewhere out of sight; and, with great deliberation, Stalky spat on to the back of a young rabbit sunning himself far down where only a cliff-rabbit could have found foot-hold. Great gray and black gulls screamed against the jackdaws; the heavy-scented acres of bloom round them were alive with low-nesting birds, singing or silent as the shadow of the wheeling hawks passed and returned; and on the naked turf across the combe rabbits thumped and frolicked.
>
> 'Whew! What a place! Talk of natural history; this is it,' said Stalky filling himself a pipe. 'Isn't it scrumptious? Good old sea!' He spat again approvingly, and was silent.
>
> McTurk and Beetle had taken out their books and were lying on their stomachs, chin in hand. The sea snored and gurgled; the birds, scattered for the moment by these new animals, returned to their businesses, and the boys read on in the rich, warm, sleepy silence."

This adventure must have happened sometime between 1878 and 1882 which spans Rudyard Kipling's time at the College. It was to be included in *Stalky and Co* (I) published in 1899, the early part of which relates his adventures at the United Services College.

The ex-railway track seen above climbing out of Westward Ho! towards the cliffs looks gentle enough, but the presence of sand lews by the side of the track suggests that, at times, trains found the slope taxing enough to have sand scattered on the rails to aid traction.

The cliffed section between Cornborough and Westward Ho! was negotiated by means of alternating cuttings and embankments. The latter provided spectacular views out over Bideford Bay. The railway was dismantled to go to France in 1917. The bare rock of the cutting are now, after nearly 100 years, well colonised by plant life, despite the exposed location. Today the old railway track between Westward Ho! and Cornborough is part of the South-West Coastal Footpath.

A history of a look-out.

On the hillside above the cutting in the main photo is an isolated look-out which has an interesting history. It is now maintained by the National Trust as part of its Kipling Tors property.

> "In December 1909 a steamer, the 'Thistlemoor', sank off Clovelly with the loss of 20 lives. Local feelings ran high as this was considered, 'a preventable loss of life', due to the lack of a good coast watch system. Within the month, after a meeting in Bideford, volunteers launched the 'North Devon Association for the Efficient Watching of our Coasts' with plans to build and man coastal look-outs of which this, the Rock Nose look-out, was one. In 1911 the Association offered the use of the look-out to the official coastguards. In January 1912, 'their objectives having been achieved', the Association was disbanded."

(From *The Cliffs of Westward Ho!* 2004)

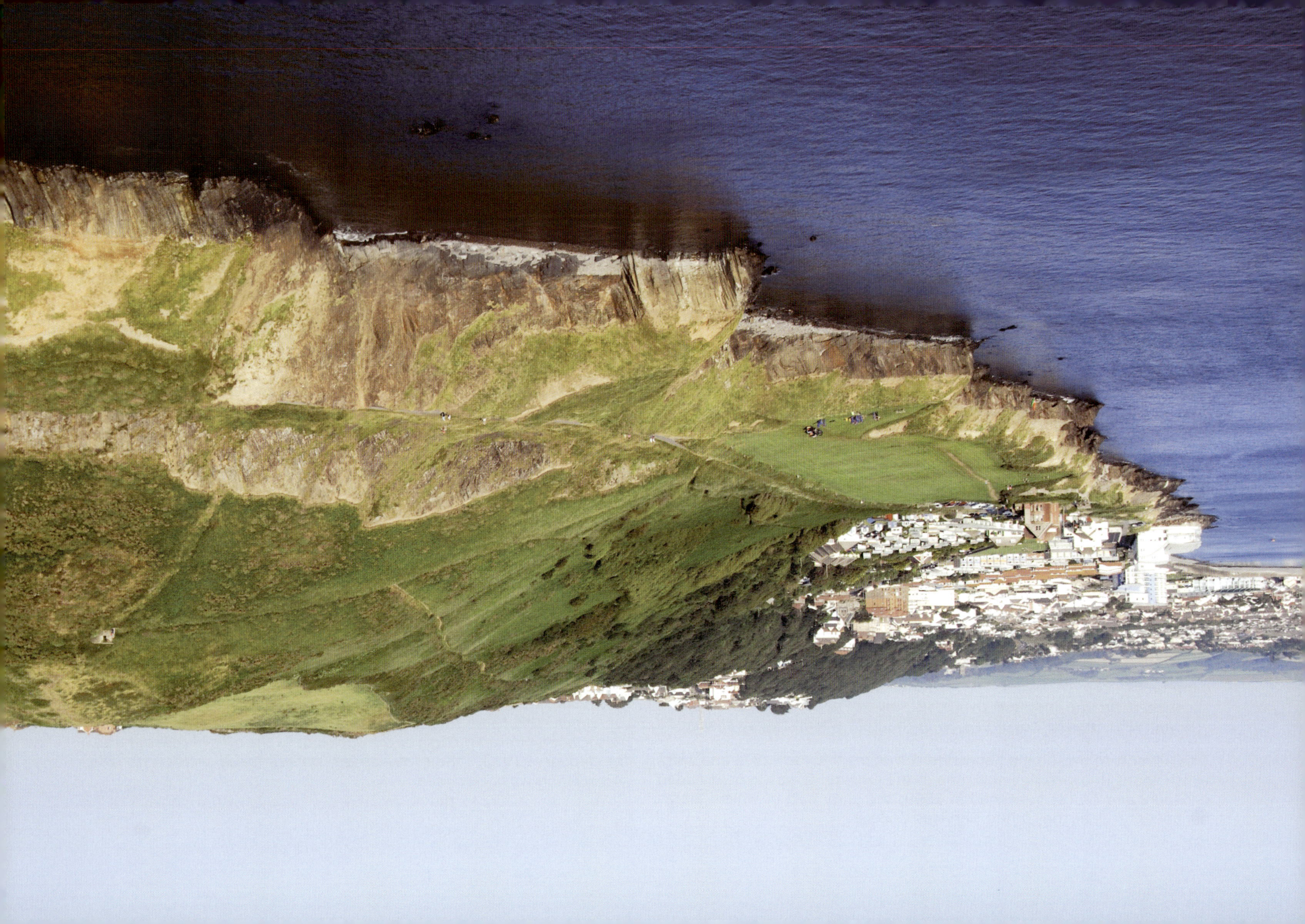

Mermaid's Pool and Rock Nose

In the air photo above, the small patch of dark rocks just breaking the sea surface on the right of the picture, are exposed at low tide as an upstanding reef of pale hard sandstone (see right). As the thick beds of this reef progress seawards from Mermaid's Pool they are periodically dislocated by faults dramatically displacing the pale reef sideways. This spendidly displayed faulting is highlighted by the dark seaweed which covers the less resistant mudstone which flanks the pale reef on either side. The photograph was taken from the Look-out roof.

I spent many days of my childhood amongst these rocks, armed with prawning net, drop-net and gaff. The deep gullies were particularly promising when an incoming tide, advancing over warm rocks, lifted the bladderwrack which hung from the sides of the gullies. Fat prawns came in with the tide. Little did I know then that the straight gullies, etched out by the sea, followed the lines of rock weakness produced by faulting. Would I have been any happier knowing that?

Sometimes I would also sit motionless gazing into Mermaid's Pool watching the rock salmon (dogfish), trapped by a falling tide and now circling restlessly awaiting the next tide. My patience was rewarded by hermit crabs emerging from shell-shelter to resume their search for detrital food. Fry and prawns eventually emerge from the hanging weeds from which colourful wrasse would peer. Green shore crabs 'crab' across the sandy pool floor. Mermaid's Pool is deep and was supposed to be bottomless. Well, mermaids are but Mermaid's Pool is not.

The Coast Turns

These air photos of this coast trigger vivid memories of a lifetime of getting to know and love this coast yet the photo (right) is really how I most remember the sea, rough, powerful and exciting - and no, I did not take this photo from my kayak but from another rock. At Rock Nose, just to the east of here, the coast turns east and quickly changes into the subdued lowland of the shores of the Taw-Torridge estuary.

The rough water on the Rock Nose section of coast has surprised me more than once, sometimes adding a little spice to the end of a day out in the kayak and, on two occasions when I funked it I landed at Cornborough, carried the kayak up to the road, and walked home to fetch the car.

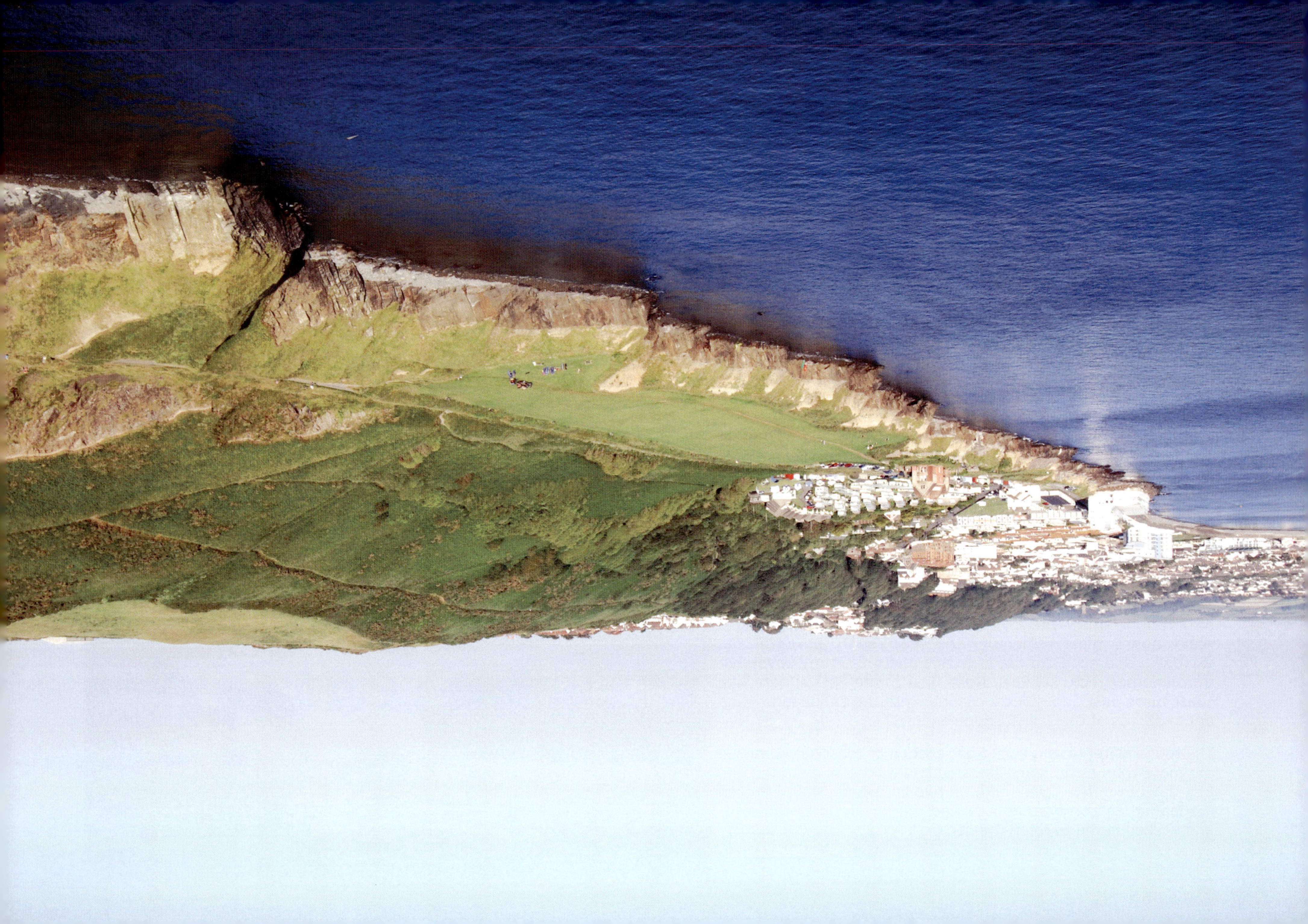

Kipling Tors and Seafield

Here, the high cliffs we have been hugging for all our flight so far, turn inland as Kipling Tors, a steep vegetated hillside which can be followed eastwards to Bone Hill (Northam) and eventually to become Appledore. Clearly these are no longer 'cliffs' as we know them. In fact, they were abandoned by the sea by a change in sea level towards 125 thousand years ago and so what we see today are the degraded remnants of an ancient cliff. We might even call it a fossil cliff-line.

This ancient cliff had at its base a fringe of grey pebbles, identical to the pebbles we have followed around Bideford Bay. In fact, we can still see these prehistoric pebbles today. On the photo above, look just above high tide mark. Note the brown rock of a mini-cliff (today's sea cliff). However, a few metres up the brown rock ends replaced by a pale coloured layer. In this pale layer we can see the pebbles of the ancient pebble beach which once fringed Kipling Tors, exposed here by present-day erosion by the sea. This ancient beach fringes the old cliff line all the way to Appledore where it is again exposed by erosion near Watertown.

If you have the chance to walk out of Westward Ho! across Seafield, the green field which tops the present mini-cliff, then with caution, you should be able to look along the cliff towards Westward Ho! and see this former pebble beach. If not, the photo (right) might suffice. Seeing this as a boy, shaped my perspective of time but I had so many seminal moments that I could not claim this made me a geomorphologist. It did however make me start to read serious things, much to the relief of my parents.

6 1

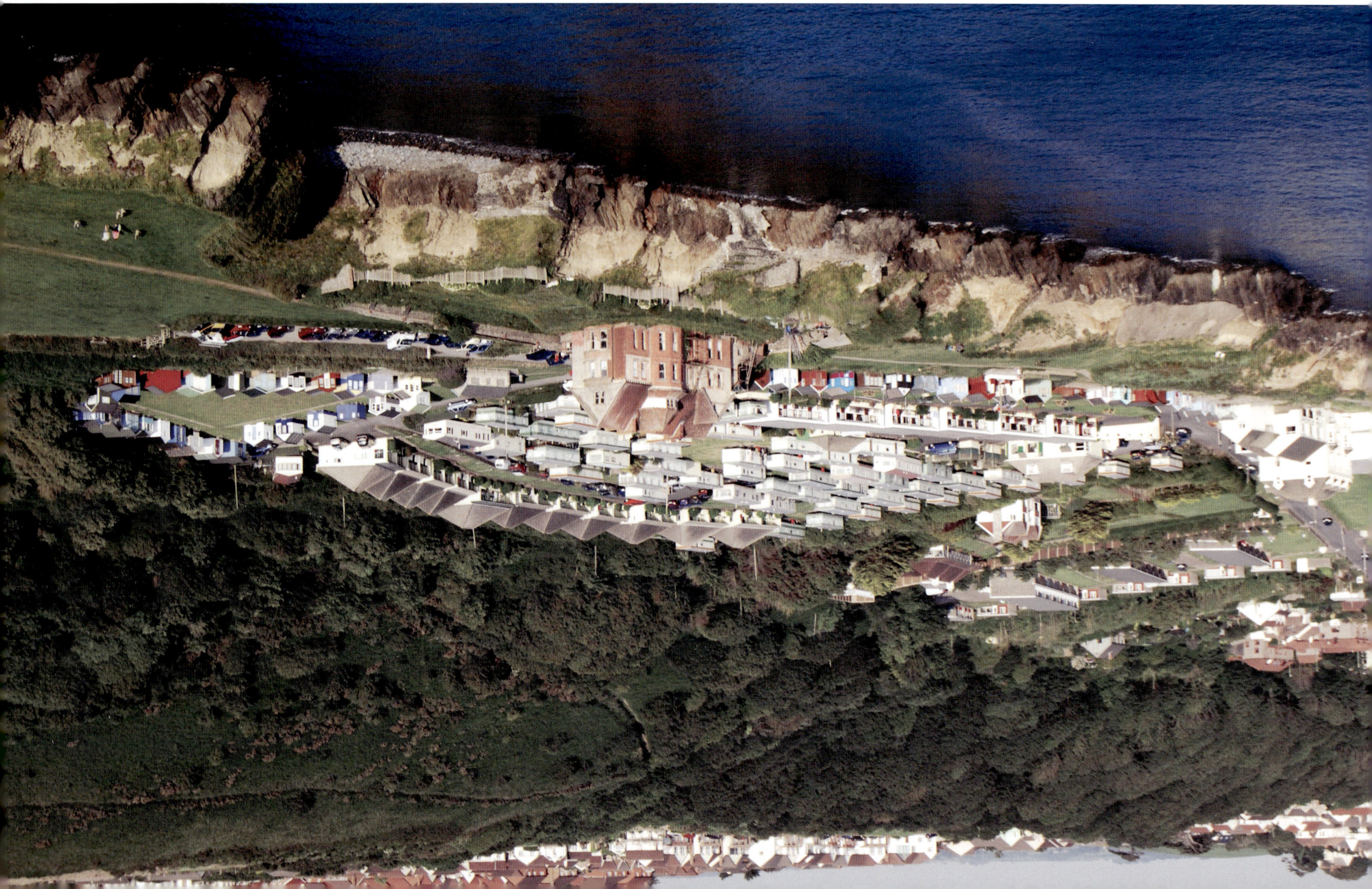

"Westward Ho Born of speculative builders in the early fifties, and christened after Kingsley's famous story, Westward Ho has grown up out of nothing into a little but rather pretty scattering of villas among golf links. At the United Services College here, Rudyard Kipling was educated. Westward Ho is fifteen minutes' railway run from Bideford."

Thus runs the printed side of the postcard (right), postmarked 1907. The artist's view on the hand-tinted card shows the view of the resort from Kipling Tors, although at that time it was still called Furze Hill, as it was in Kipling's time at the United Services College. The hill was renamed Kipling Tors in 1927 when it was thrown open to the public but with an entrance fee, 50% of which was to be given to the 'Coastal Protection Fund'. At the base of the picture postcard is written "Kingsley's Country Westward Ho." (Note no !).

The red brick building in the photo above (Seafield) was one of the *'rather pretty scattering of villas'* described on the back of the postcard. A previous handwritten postcard (on page 95) described Westward Ho! in 1911 as *'a very grand place'* - and so it must have appeared at that time. Seafield was built circa 1885 as a summer residence for a London Banker. The next villa to the east was Merley House, the large white house on the left hand side of the photo above. The general plan of the village at that time shows a spacious scattering of villas, hotels and colleges. However, the speculative commercial venture 'The Northam Burrows Hotel and Villas Company' was not a success and in 1907 most of the building and land associated with the Company was sold off.

Subsequently, many of the Victorian buildings were replaced by more modern 'speculative building'. Seafield House still endures although in a rather sorry state. Nikolaus Pevsner in 1952 wrote scathingly about Victorian Westward Ho! and this may have reflected architectural opinion of his time but today seems almost comical in its self-assurance. Surviving Victorian buildings stand aloft from subsequent development, the tide of which has spread in every direction and now laps against Seafield House.

The Westward Ho! of my youth I remember as a marvellous place in which to grow up, and it probably still is. Within ten minutes you can be in the sea, on the sands, walking Northam Burrows, rock pooling on the shore or walking on the cliffs. Looking at these air photos I must admit that, aesthetically, it is probably better to be in the village looking out at fine landscapes rather than looking at the village from the outside.

Thinking about that, I looked up some of my collection of published descriptions of Westward Ho! One striking thing was that at the time of its early development, already established watering places would spend much time denigrating any resort which was seen as a potential competitor. I have a 130-page book on Swanage to hand, published in 1890. Much of the book praises Swanage for its 'resources as an invigorating health resort'. It also addresses its competitors and for each, provides a few lines of disparagement. Overleaf, I quote some Swanage entries and other published critical descriptions most of which should be read with a pinch of salt!

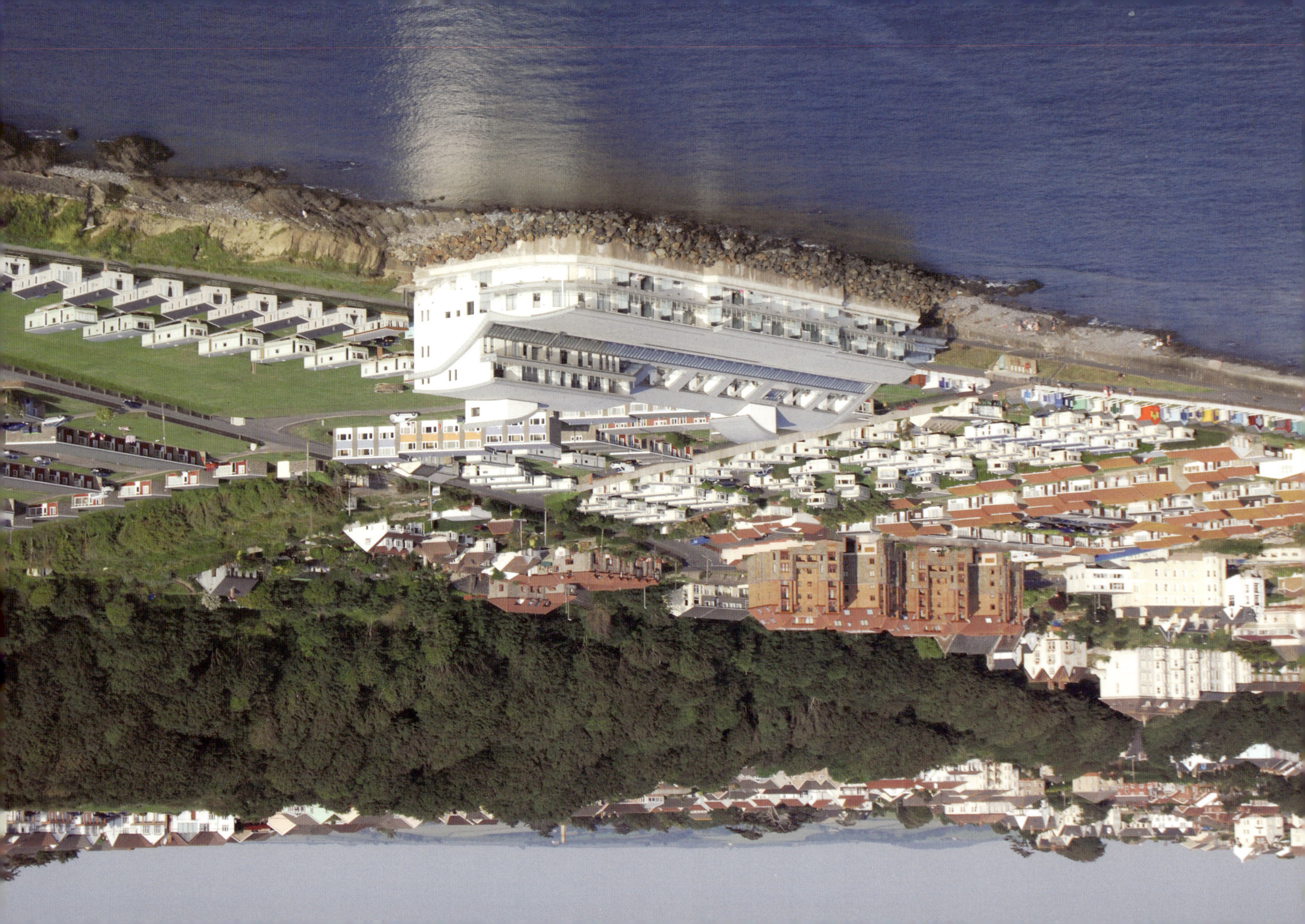

Westward Ho!   What the critics have said: NKJ 6

1864 Charles Kingsley, dismayed by the prospect of his beauty spot being overcome by a rash of speculative building, unleashed by his successful novel, wrote mournfully to Dr W H Ackland, a Bideford friend.

"How goes on the Northam scheme for spoiling that beautiful place with hotels and villas? I suppose it must be – if there is a demand let it be supplied – but you will frighten away the seapies and defile the Pebble Ridge with chicken bones and sandwich scraps. The Universe is growing Cockney, and men like me must look out for a planet to live without fear of railways and villa projectors."

1889 "Punch" 5th October 1889.

Westward Ho! "Here is a Kingsley Inn, Kingsley tradesmen none of them apparently doing a big business. A Kingsley village, as it were, in a very poor way, but an idea about it of trying to live up its reputation and failing; a desolate looking Kingsley College, without any Kingsley students, so we were informed; and as part and parcel of the building, is a Kingsley College Chapel, but very few collegians, if any, to attend its services. The houses about seem to have been planned by different architects, each one of whom tried to outdo the other in building something uglier and drearier than the last. 'Oho!' a fresh architect seems to have said to himself, as he viewed the most recent work of a rival, 'he thought he could make a dull and dreary building did he? Bah! I'll show 'em what dullness and dreariness mean;' and at once he set to work to do it, and succeeded."

1890 from **SWANAGE, its history and resources as an invigorating health resort**

WESTWARD HO!: "a place on the north-west coast of Devon, where the sun can only shine nine months in the year, owing to the height of the cliffs ... Westward Ho! has little to recommend it beyond the exhilarating climate, and for this reason a college [The United Services College] has been established there for hardening boys intended to battle with the treacherous climate of our Eastern Empire in after-life."

VENTNOR: "one great disadvantage is that it is overrun with invalids of every description, which is very depressing."

BRIGHTON: "Brighton, now called "London-super-Mare" is simply a fashionable watering place, over-crowded in every way, with nothing to commend it as a residence for invalids; and I much question whether the system of drainage is good."

WORTHING: "It possesses a clay soil. but there is always a peculiar effluvium there, at least I have frequently observed this when the tide is low, which makes me question whether such can be healthy in itself."

CLIFTON: "In Clifton the air is too dry, from the fact that by its situation the limestone rock absorbs nearly all the moisture."

1952 Nikolaus Pevsner
The Buildings of England: North Devon

Westward Ho!. The landmarks of 1870 are all still there, monuments to the nadir of light-heartedness in English architecture, and therefore singularly unsuited to a seaside resort. The yellow brick of N Devon does not help matters either.

2008 Excerpts from WESTWARD HO! area design statement (Torridge District Council) November 2008 Community Planning and Development Services. Townscape Character appraisal.

"Steep wooded cliffs with Victorian terraces 'set in' to the escarpment provide a sense of 'enclosure' enhancing character.

Large areas of the public realm in the village centre have a tired or 'neglected' appearance with visually intrusive building frontages and activities; including promenade, village green / square and the area around the slipway.

Height and massing of recent development (e.g. Nassau Court and Ocean Park apartments) is incongruous with their settings.

New housing on top of the escarpment changes the nature of the hilltop and creates a sense that this feature is diminishing.

Elsewhere much recent housing development is single storey creating a rather 'flat' appearance with poor sense of enclosure making the area seem exposed.

Need to ensure that development is sufficiently high to complement the escarpment setting, but taller buildings right on the seafront sever rather than frame visual relationships with the sea and coastal area - compromising expansive views."

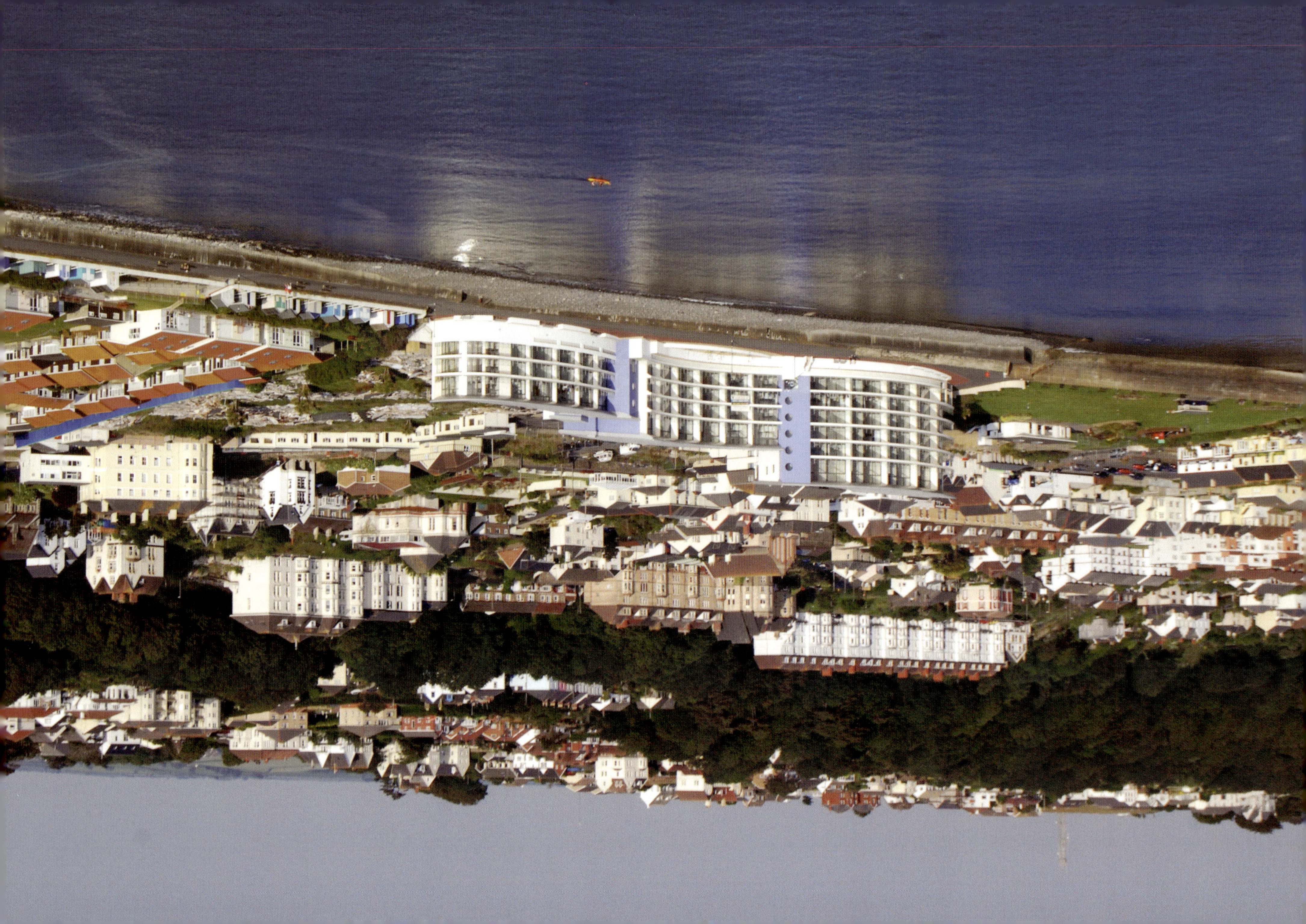

Westward Ho! Kipling at the United Services College, the long white building with red chimneys (above left). 'Twelve bleak houses by the shore!'

Rudyard Kipling was born in India in 1865 but like most English families serving in India, at the age of five Rudyard was sent to England to be educated. In January 1878 Kipling was admitted to the United Services College, a school founded a few years earlier to prepare 'poorer' boys for the British Army. The school was aggressively athletic, competitive and physically 'masculine' with corporal punishment the order of the day. Stalky and Co (1899) opens with poetry, two verses of which reflect his early reactions:

> *"Western wind and open surge*
> *Tore us from our mothers;*
> *Flung us on a naked shore*
> *(Twelve bleak houses by the shore!*
> *Seven summers by the shore!)*
> *'Mid two hundred brothers.*
>
> *There we met with famous men*
> *Set in office o'er us.*
> *And they beat on us with rods--*
> *Faithfully with many rods--*
> *Daily beat us on with rods--*
> *For the love they bore us!"*

Attracted by the book's early Westward Ho! setting I read *Stalky and Co* as a young teenager. I took a schoolboy delight in the japes that Rudyard's pals got up to, despite the vindictive humiliation meted out to his adversaries, both other pupils and staff. Rereading it 63 years later I had rather a different take. Rudyard, a sensitive precocious intellectual is fighting to retain his boyhood independence in a system designed to enforce conformity. He and his boyhood mates fight an often devious battle with authority, avoiding events such as organised sport sometimes retreating to a secret hide-out where they can relax, read and smoke. Finding this lair is described on page 99. Kipling returned to India in 1882 and was not to publish Stalky and Co until 17 years had passed, 1899.

Problems with the sea Westward Ho! has experienced problems in its relationship with the sea from the time when the first houses were constructed on what was previously lowland open farmland. In retrospect the reasons for these problems are clear. Firstly, there was little appreciation that parts of the resort were being built on a shore which was already experiencing rapid coastal erosion. Both the Pebble Ridge and the soft cliffs were being eaten by the sea at an alarming rate. Secondly, the Victorian era was one of over-confidence fed by successful empire building, the great advances in engineering (just think of Isambard Kingdom Brunel) and the belief that nature could and should be subjugated for the good of mankind - Westward Ho! Pier is a good example of this.

Westward Ho! like many aspiring coastal watering places, once had a pleasure pier where paddle steamers which plied the coastal resorts of the Bristol Channel would call. This pier was constructed just west of the above photo, close to Merley House. It was opened to much acclaim in 1871. Mr Wilson, as an engineer responsible in part for the construction of the pier was asked to address the Society of Engineers on the subject of Westward Ho! Pier. This he did on March 1st 1875.

> *"Works in the sea are for many reasons attractive to the engineer, but there is no doubt that in such undertakings he has to contend with an enemy of enormous power in the mighty waters. There are however, some who are never so happy as when they feel they are coping with an antagonist whose strength is a match for their own, and with some chance of success, and who like Alexander, would weep if they felt that they had no more worlds to conquer. To such if given to bring into subjugation the forces of nature, and even to say to the sea, 'Thus far shalt you come and no further'."*
>
> (J W Wilson March 1875)

"Within five years of Mr Wilson's address, Westward Ho! pier was in ruins being so badly damaged by storms that in 1880 the remains had to be dismantled. At low tide the cast iron stumps are still visible, a memorial to Victorian optimism."

(from 'Westward Ho! Against the Sea' *7*).　　I J 7 1

110

Westward Ho! Sea wall

Between 1928 and 1931 a vertical sea wall was built in front of a soft cliff of sand and clay to protect several terraces which were under immediate threat of destruction by the sea.

The sea wall in 1960

I had an early interest in Westward Ho! sea wall not least because our cottage was only some 70 metres behind the wall. When my mother anticipated a stormy high tide she would remove the best crockery from the dresser, as waves hitting the wall would shake the cottage enough to rattle the plates. The front room fire would hiss as spray descended the chimney. Not having television, we would collect in the rear bedroom to view the show. The slab-like wall would send up spectacular sheets of water and on occasion completely overtop the wall to send a secondary wave over the promenade and into our field advancing towards our cottage. Very exciting stuff!

Behind this wave is the sea wall!

The arcade, right, is just behind the sea wall, seen here before and after a high tide. Look at the lettering. It suggests this is not the first time this has happened. In winter wooden shutters defend against waves and pebbles.

When I developed a more academic interest in the seawall, I would trawl old postcard stalls in local markets for photos giving a good view of the clay and sand cliff against which the sea wall was built. Unfortunately the bulk of these photos were of holiday groups with only a hint of my '*real*' interest behind them! The photo below was an exception, for there was my mother (second from right), perhaps with boyfriends? She would have been on a day trip from Torrington where she lived. Dated 1925, this was before she met my father and 12 years before I was born.

Above: In 1982-3 the most exposed section of the wall was protected by an apron of rocks (rock armour). I took the photo as I arrived home from a day at sea, to find no gentle sandy beach exposed. However, my yellow Umnak kayak (see page 53) is based on an Aleutian Islands design and will ride up onto the Pebble Ridge just as well as ice flows. Ride your wave; run aground; pull the spray deck clear; grasp the coaming; leap out before the backwash sets in - grab the kayak. I even get a flurry of applause from the sea wall!

FAQ: How powerful are these waves and where do they come from? I hope this helps.

Bathtime (after Hokusai)

"Where on Hartland's tempest-furrowed shore
Breaks the long swell from Labrador."

Many years ago when I first read the lines, left, and quoted by Hoskins in 1954, I thought of it a poetic fancy. Only later did I recognise how true it was.

"Winds blowing over the surface of the water create waves, transferring part of the energy of the wind into the waves. . . . Once created, waves will spread out from their energy source. For example a storm far out in the Atlantic [Labrador?] can create waves which, two days later, will arrive on the shore at Westward Ho! as large breakers, even though there is no wind blowing here at the time.

This principle can be demonstrated the next time you lie back in your bath. By wiggling your big toe, muscular energy is transferred from you to the water. The agitated water will travel up the length of the bath in the form of waves, eventually breaking against your chin, or other obstructions it meets on the way. Your chin may be regarded as Westward Ho! beach." (7)

OMG. Once a teacher always a teacher.

"Waves four metres high, arriving on one kilometre of beach at Westward Ho! every eight seconds, each has the energy of 32 lorries of 33 tonnes doing 70 m.p.h. In a 24 hour day this is the equivalent of 345,600 lorries." (7)

"...the wind-sloped trees, the dark levels of the Burrows, and the white line of breakers falling nine-deep along the Pebble Ridge.

Rudyard Kipling

112

718

Westward Ho! Pebble Ridge A problem which immediately confronted the developers was the unrecognised speed of coastal retreat. Physically demonstrating this in the field proved a rewarding little exercise for visiting groups.

In this little exercise, old dated photos, taken along the ridge crest looking towards Westward Ho! were aligned with old buildings and so the line of sight of the photographer and hence the ridge crest at that time could be worked out. The exercise ended with banners being displayed and the retreat measured. At this location it suggested that the ridge had retreated 150 metres between 1861 and 1932 (averaging over two metres a year).

1962: Pebble Ridge breached by storm. Burrows flooded. Bulldozers seal breach.

1974: Storm overtops the full length of Pebble Ridge. Burrows flooded.

1994: Storm overtops ridge. Flooding.

114

Northam Burrows The Burrows today is largely a swathe of coastal grassland used for grazing animals, playing golf, walking the dog, riding horses, birdwatching or simply taking a brisk walk over coastal grassland. This is drained by ditches directing water towards the Appledore corner of the Burrows and issuing into the Skern. Northam Burrows as a Country Park is used extensively by the local community and holiday makers. Both the Pebble Ridge and the Country Park are designated SSSIs. Management attempts to strike a balance between public use and the needs of conservation and preservation. Recent erosional events make 'striking a balance' even more difficult. However, the threat of inundation has been a topic of discussion for over 160 years.

Northam Burrows circa 1797 Few knew what this landscape looked like before the Burrows were reclaimed. However, in 2002 a painting by Thomas Girtin, which had previously been mis-catalogued as a view of Porlock, was recognised as being of Northam Burrows and Bideford Bay looking towards Clovelly and Hartland Point (see below). It looks as if Girtin made this watercolour 'sketch' from the Look-out on the flanks of Staddon Hill. Those who know Appledore can probably just pick it out on the air photo above. Northam Burrows then appeared as a coastal marsh of meandering streams and lakes, before straight ditches enhanced drainage to improve grazing, but the lowering of the water table worked to the disadvantage of wetland plants, today protected by the SSSI status of the Burrows.

Beyond the Burrows, the wisp of smoke against the dark hillside is from one of two farmsteads that occupied the land which some 66 years later was to become Westward Ho! On the left is Northam Church and closer is smoke from Diddywell. Closer still, in the trees, is Watertown.

This is a very well executed and accurate sketch. When Thomas Girtin died in 1802, JMW Turner said of him, *"If Tom had lived, I would have starved"*.

"He (Amyas Leigh) walked down to the pebble ridge, where the surges of the bay have defeated their own fury, by rolling up in the course of ages a rampart of gray boulder-stones, some two miles long, as cunningly curved, and smoothed, and fitted, as if the work had been done by human hands, which protects from the high tides of spring and autumn a fertile sheet of smooth alluvial turf.

Sniffing the keen salt air like a young sea-dog, he stripped and plunged into the breakers, and dived, and rolled, and tossed about the foam with stalwart arms, till he heard himself hailed from off the shore."

(Charles Kingsley *'Westward Ho!'* 1855).

8 6 1 C

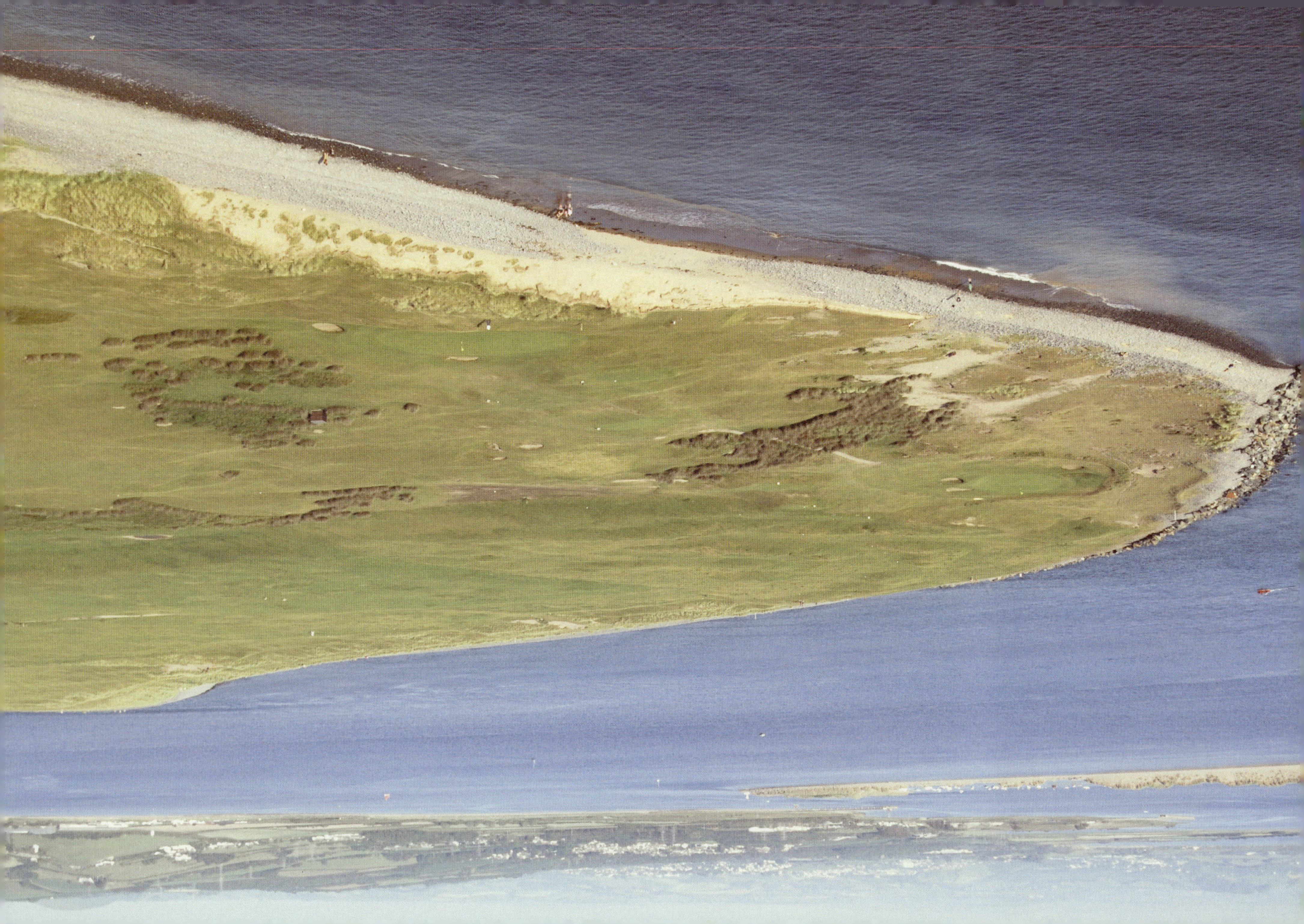

The estuary mouth The northern tip of the Burrows. Far left is the Taw, to the right the Torridge, meeting in Appledore Pool before flowing left to meet the bar, usually marked by a line of breakers, a realm of shifting shoals and sand banks.

"The hills...in softly rounded knolls... sink into the wide expanse of hazy flats, rich salt-marshes, and rolling sand-hills, where Torridge joins her sister Taw, and both together flow quietly towards the broad surges of the bar, and the everlasting thunder of the long Atlantic swell."   (Charles Kingsley, 'Westward Ho!' 1855)

Estuary mouths are very dynamic coastal environments often with spits which periodically grow, only to be breached by waves at their narrow neck, then reform sometime later. These days authorities can usually think of reasons why a spit should not be allowed to be breached. At Grey Sand Hill (above) the shore has been reinforced by rock armour to prevent loss of land at this point. Coastal erosion here has been a serious problem at this site for many years:

1861: "A Proposal for Securing the whole of Northam Burrows from the encroachment of the Seas' Rev. I Gossett, writes to his Northam parishioners:

"I suggest for the consideration of the Parishioners that the time has come when, if something be not done to secure the Burrows from the ruinous encroachments of the sea, the difficulty and expense of doing so will be enormously increased. The Sand Hills, the continuation of what was once Gray Sand Hill, attacked by the tidal waters in rear as well as in front, are rapidly giving way, and there seems every probability of a much larger portion of the Burrows being covered, eaten into and seriously damaged by the spring-tides. From a survey and map made for the parish by Mr Cuming, in 1855, it appeared that 65 acres were then already lost, and that 96 acres more were then rendered valueless.....in all probability ten more years will witness the destruction of at least half the Burrows, unless the evil be promptly met and remedied without delay." **M**

The Admiralty chart of 1832 shows Grey Sand spit as broken into sand/gravel islets whilst Crow Point spit does not exist.

Instructions for sailing ships in distress crossing the bar. (Captain H M Denham R.N. 1839).

"...all but vessels of a certain draught must bide the tide, and may therefore be caught by one of the sudden and violent N.W. gales which are so frequent on this coast, and thus be forced into the breakers. If any control can be exerted on a vessel in such a case, the master should do his best to urge her as much as possible towards the beach, under Northam Burrows, as a life-boat is kept in readiness on that side, which in the eighteen months after it was established, saved eleven lives."

1865 Townsend M. Hall addressing a meeting at the Westward Ho! Hotel
"On their north eastern side, the Northam Burrows have no pebble breakwater to protect them; but a range of sand hills once formed a very effective, though as it has proved, temporary defence. Since 1861 the tidal currents have cut no less than 20 gaps into the remaining parts of the hills....so rapid is the destruction in progress, that if for five years more it goes on unchecked at the rate it has done for the last ten years, not only will the common be further diminished by one half, but the parishioners will know to their cost that the evil will have grown too vast for the parish of Northam to cope with."   **M**

Fast-forward to the early 1970s. The green pasture in the picture above hides an inexplicably bad decision in the 1970s to infill the low area behind Grey Sand Spit with refuse composed largely of domestic rubbish. This dump was not finally closed until 1993, the waste being covered with soil, landscaped and grassed over. However, by 1978 the shore was being actively eroded and rock armour was emplaced and added to periodically ever since. Of course, this story is not over yet!

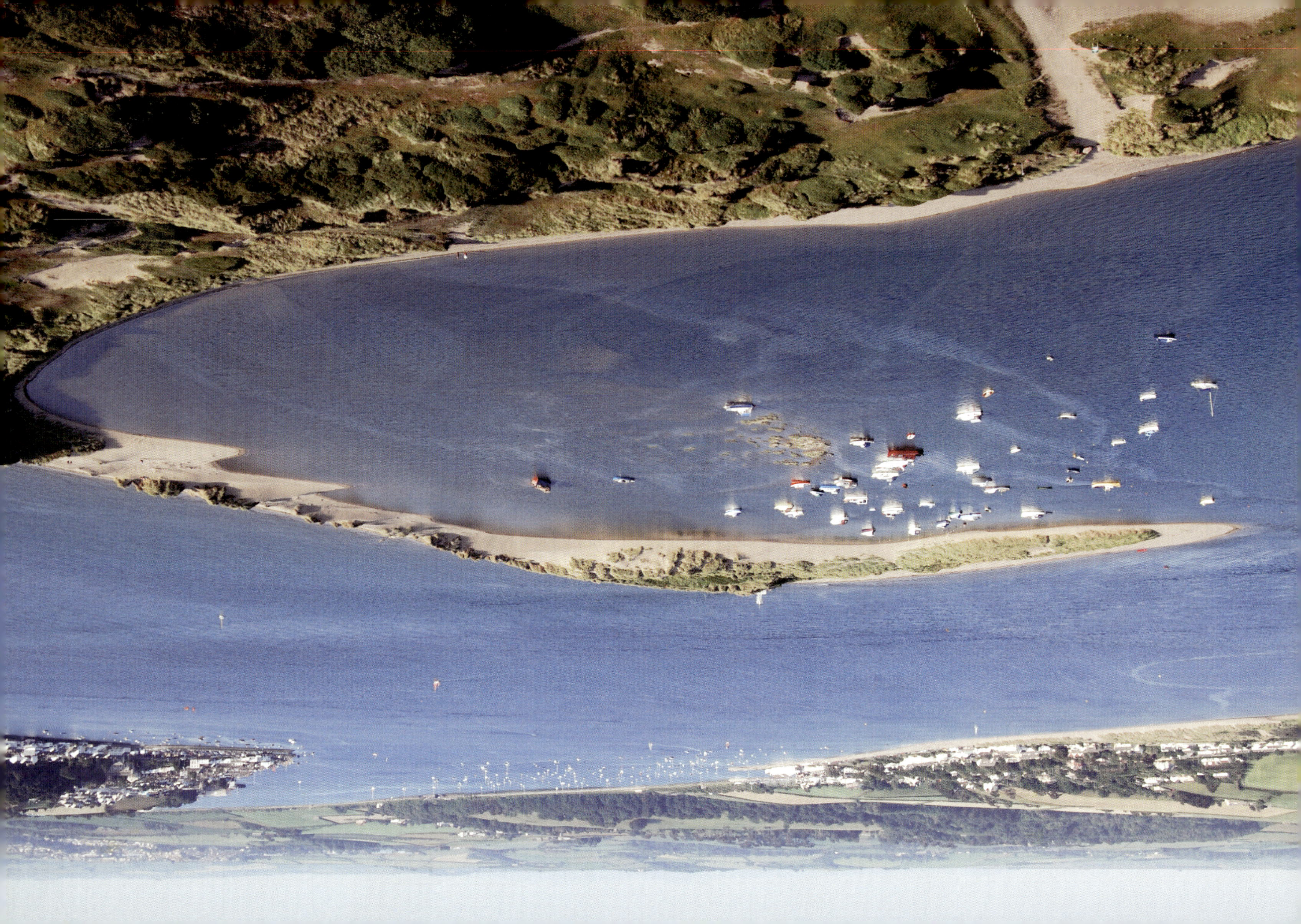

left to right: **Taw - Instow - Crow Point - Torridge - West Appledore**

Crow Point on the east side of the estuary is a prominent recurving spit with a narrow neck but does not appear on 19th century maps such as the Admiralty Chart of 1832 (page 117). The neck has been reinforced in the past but clearly by 2009 was being overtopped by waves on high tides. Should nature be allowed to takes its course?

CROW ISLAND and the sand barges

Sand barges being loaded on the Crow in the 1960s. A barge would float down the Taw just after high tide to ground on the Crow. It then had until the next incoming tide to float it off again to catch the flood tide back up the Taw. The barges were filled to the brim with sand or gravel. So full were they that their gunnels seemed only an inch or so above the river. Their one cylinder four-stroke engine made a distinctive, evocative sound, a 'Put, tut, tut, tut, Put', which would travel a great distance over the water on a calm quiet evening. At low tide, kayaking in the Taw meant that there was always a choice of water leads to follow (see below) and a bad choice, with a lead that was too shallow to follow through, would result in a portage. It always had an air of gambling. Drifting with the tide, it is easy to be mesmerised by the patterns of sand and water.

Taw at low tide. Yelland Power Station in the distance

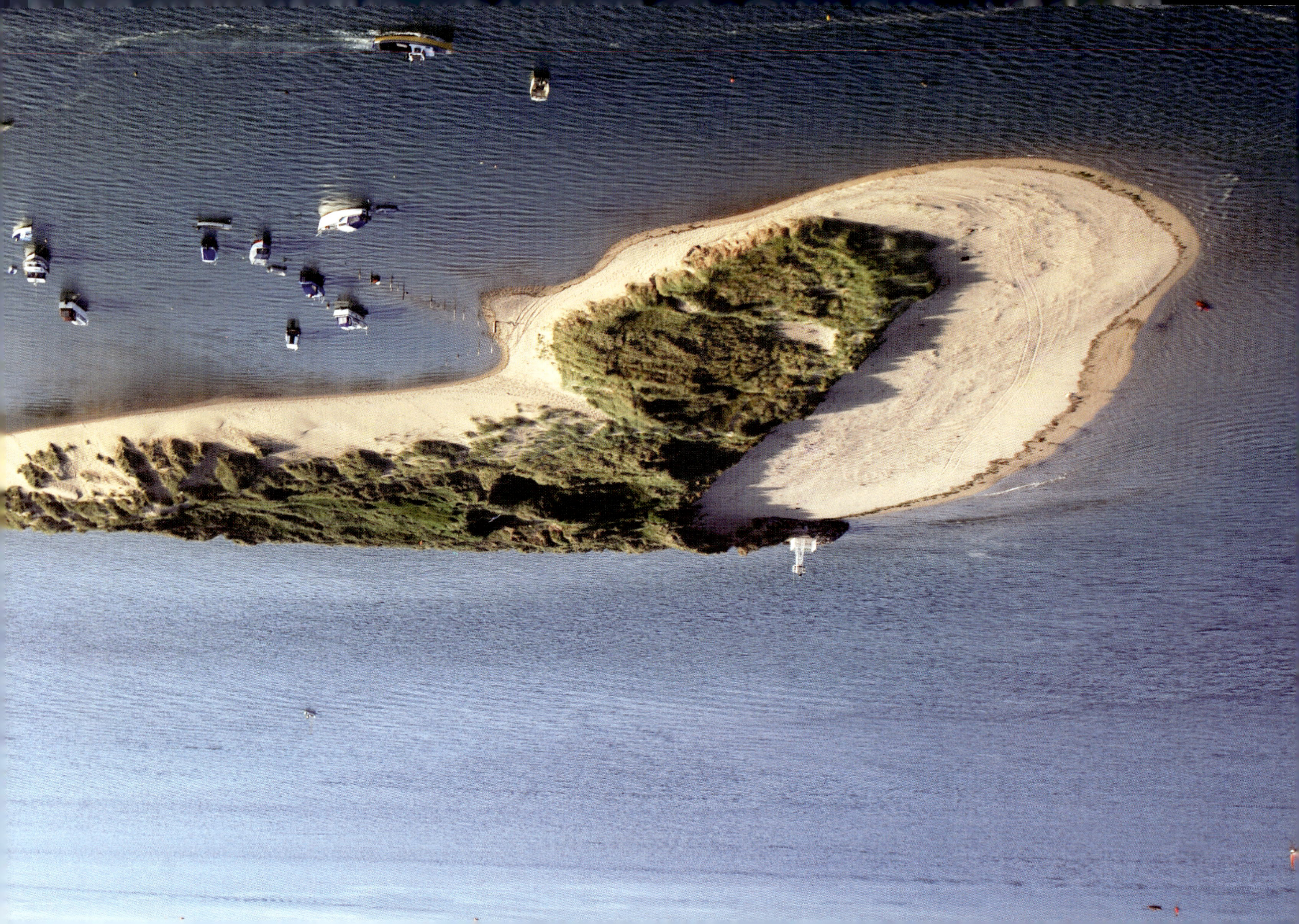

CROW ISLAND and the estuary mouth

"The tide took them to the spit of gravel, crowned by sandhills bound with marram grass, called Crow Island, and here they left the water for a ragrowster. While the cubs were rolling and biting, Tarka and White-tip played the game of searching and pretending not to find. They galloped up the sandhills to slide to the hollows again. They picked up sticks, empty shells of skate's eggs, old bones and feathers of sea birds, corks from the jetsam of high tide, and tossed them in their paws. They hid in the spines of the tussocks, and jumped out at each other."

"The lighthouse beam shone on the wet sands by the water, and across the Pool the lights of the village lay like wind-blown embers. Craa-leek, cur-lee-eek! The curlews saw them as they swam the shallow water to the Shrarshook. White-tip and Tarka ate mussels down by the black-and-white Pulley buoy, and the cubs followed them to the lower reaches."
('Tarka the Otter'. Henry Williamson 1927)

The lower reaches - Zulu Bank. A rather large picture perhaps showing not that much. Yet it does have the feel of the uneasy isolation one experiences, particular when, in a kayak, your eyes are only two feet from the sea. Most of the landscape is beyond the horizon. The thin white line is the bar or what you can see of it. Yet you can hear "the everlasting thunder of the long Atlantic swell". The sand shivers and disappears disconcertingly fast beneath the incoming tide. I turn for home earlier than intended.

L 8 1

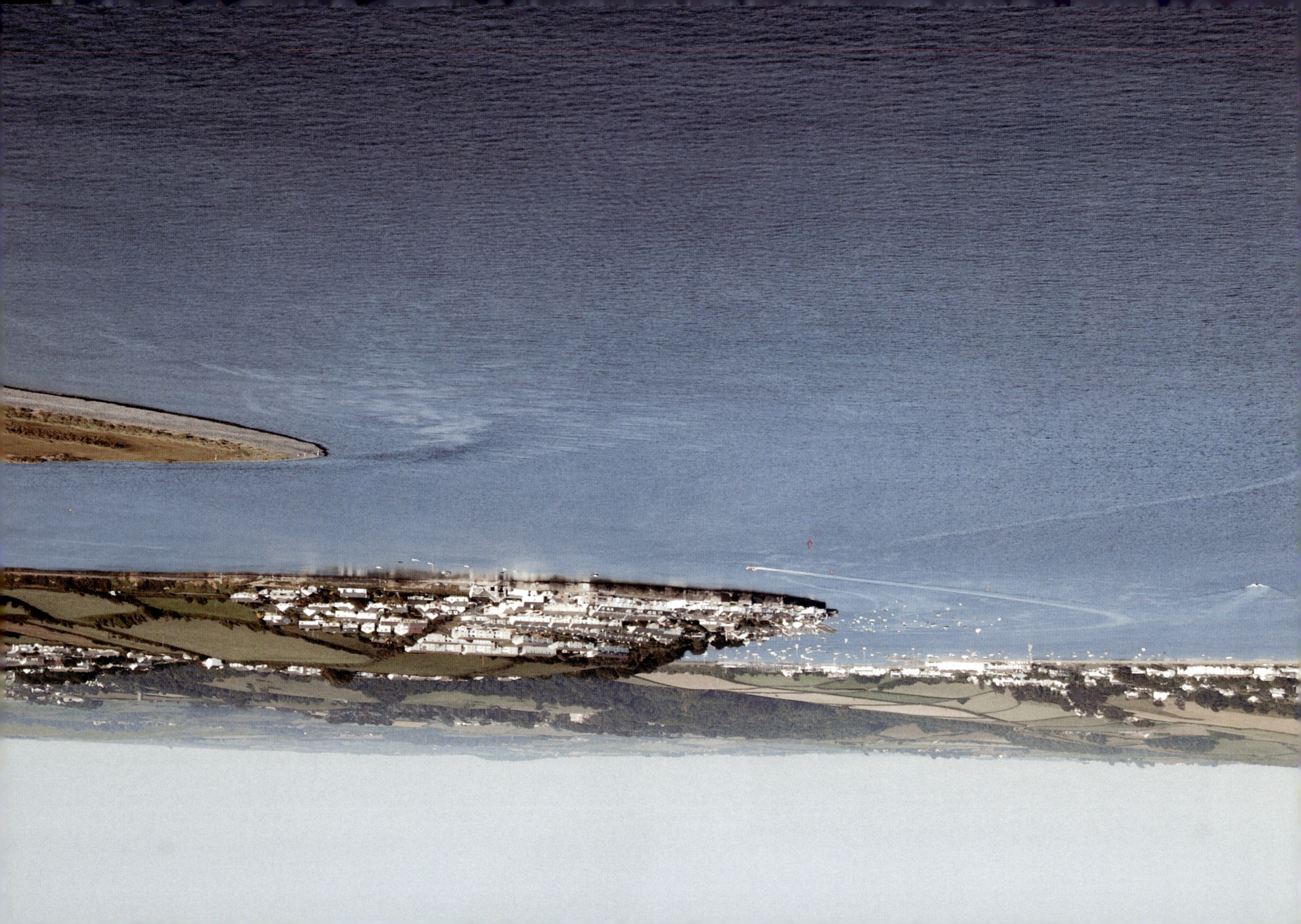

Instow - Torridge - Appledore Pool - West Appledore - Skern - Grey Sand Spit

Crossing the bar was always a hazardous venture in the days of sail. Murdoch Mackenzie had this advice in 1772:

"Before you run in for the Bar you should bring Baggy Point which is the northern most point of Barnstaple Bay to bear North. which bearing from Baggy will lead in the channel over the Bar: continue to steer South from Baggy, till a Perch, a pole serving as a navigation mark, that stands on a sandy hillock on your larboard hand on going in, bears East: then steer for that Perch till you have four fathoms of water when you will have passed over the Bar, and in all probability will meet with a Pilot; then steer SE.bS. taking your soundings from the sand along the shore on your starboard hand on going in, til you are abreast of Grison [Greysand?] Bay, where you may anchor, or may run your ship aground upon clean sand with great safety [Skern?].

Appledore lies about a mile ESE-wards of Grison. The largest merchant ships may ride afloat in the Pool, but ships that can take the ground had better haul ashore on the sand at Appledore than lie afloat, for they have hardly room to swing in the Pool, and spring tides when strongest run 4 miles an hour. Vessels that draw 13 or 14 feet water may get to Bideford Quay at high spring tide."

Above: West Appledore, perched over the river.
Below: Across the salt marsh and Skern towards Appledore 1996.

"Appledore up to this time (pre-1914) had been a flourishing little seaside town. It was a fine sight to see forests of masts and sails going over the bar after Christmas. Sometimes up to 100 little vessels in one tide would leave the port."

All the sailors with few exceptions, in those days joined the Royal Naval Reserve and as there was a training battery at Appledore it was the custom to do some drill between voyages . . . This helped to keep these little ships going, as the R.N.R. money subsidised the low wages they could pay.

Many a time, as a youngster, I have seen a crowd of sailors on Appledore Quay early in the morning watching the bar and the weather. If they couldn't get over the bar, they would hastily put on their naval uniform and be off to the battery at West Appledore."

(W J Slade. *Out of Appledore* 1959).

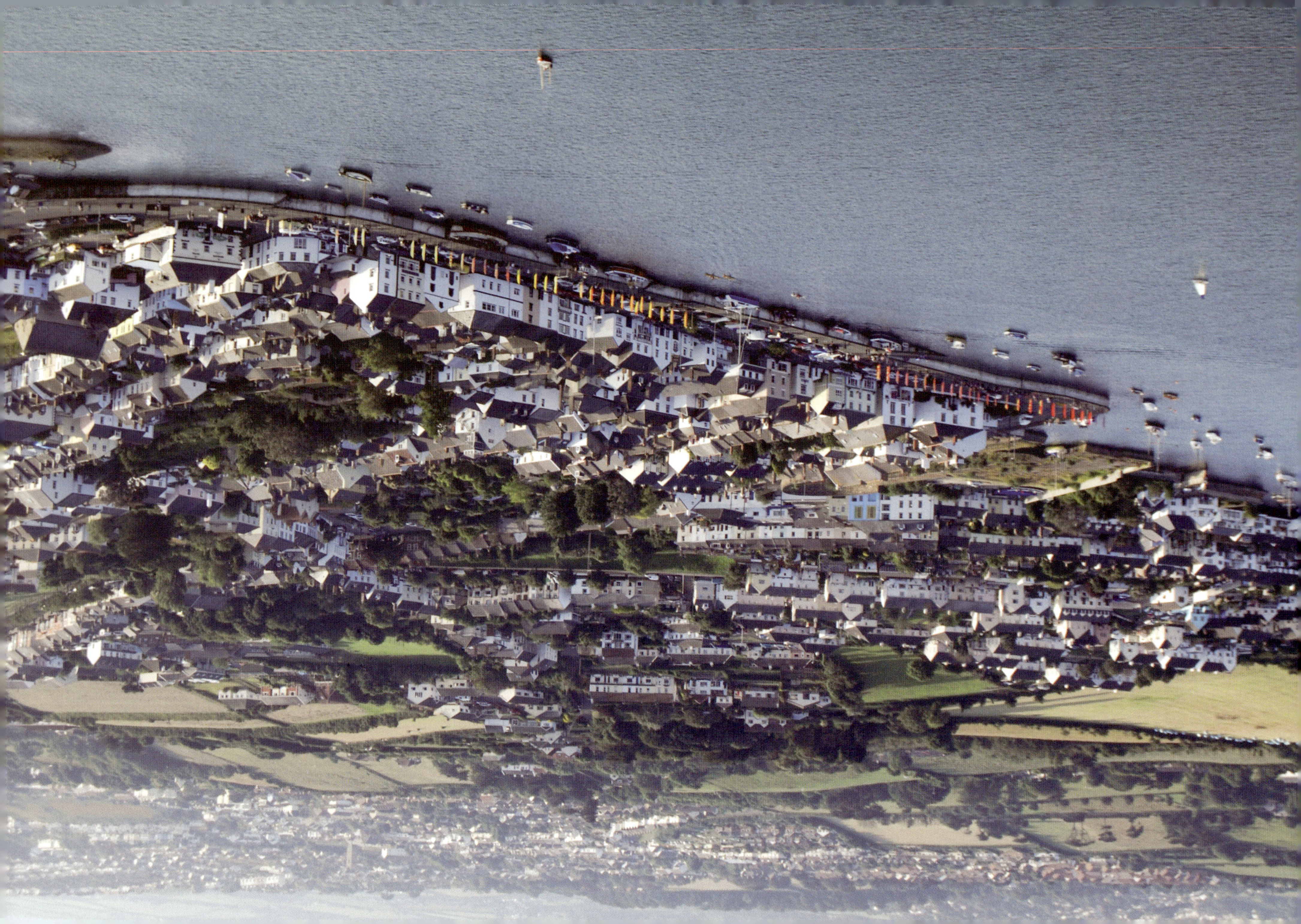

Appledore Quay 23rd June 2009 and 1819.

DOP

A 1819 view from the Instow shore, of Appledore, both east and west, based on a painting by George Shepherd.

> *Appledore is a delightful unspoilt village at the meeting place of beautiful Taw and Torridge estuaries. The delicate colouring of the estuary, of the Braunton Burrows, and of the hills beyond, is matched by the colour-wash everywhere in the village. The streets are narrow, many of the houses old; some are certainly Elizabethan.*
>
> W G Hoskins.

Well, that sounds a pleasant note to end on, except that there is such a strong maritime heritage to this little port that there is not room here to do justice to that. However, there are two sources of further reading which you should find of interest: an illustrated history of Appledore by David Carter (O) and the North Devon Maritime History Museum which is situated in Appledore (Oden Road). They have published a selection of books on local maritime history (P).

Peter Keene
October 2013

Further Reading on the North-West Devon Coast with Thematic Trails

1 **CLASSIC LANDFORMS OF THE NORTH DEVON COAST** Peter Keene. Geographical Association 1986, 2nd edition 1996. Re-printed by Thematic Trails 2005. ISBN 978-0-948444-58-6. 48 pages (A5). 29 illustrations.

2 **STRAWBERRY WATER TO MARSLAND MOUTH** Peter Keene. Thematic Trails 1990. ISBN 978-0-948444-06-7. 40 pages (A5). 30 illustrations.

3 **THE CLIFFS OF HARTLAND QUAY** Peter Keene. Thematic Trails 2006. ISBN 978-0-948444-46-3. 48 Pages (A5). 53 illustrations in full colour.

4 **GEOLOGY AT HARTLAND QUAY** Chris Cornford & Alan Childs. Thematic Trails 1989. ISBN 978-0-948444-12-8. 40 Pages (A5). 47 illustrations.

5 **BUCKS MILLS people and place** John Bradbeer. Thematic Trails 2011. ISBN 978-0-948444-56-2. 36 pages (A5). 32 illustrations in full colour.

6 **THE CLIFFS OF WESTWARD HO! a sense of time** Peter Keene. Thematic Trails 2004. ISBN 978-0-948444-35-7. 52 pages (A5). 70 colour illustrations.

7 **WESTWARD HO! AGAINST THE SEA** Peter Keene. Thematic Trails 1997. ISBN 978-0-948444-34-0. 48 pages (A5). 24 illustrations.

8 **NORTHAM BURROWS, estuary environments** Janet and Peter Keene. Thematic Trails 1997. ISBN 978-0-948444-33-3. 48 pages (A5). 30 illustrations.

9 **BRAUNTON BURROWS ECOLOGY TRAIL** Janet Keene. Thematic Trails 1996. 2nd Edition 2003. ISBN 978-0-948444-30-2. A5. 47 pages (A5). 30 illustrations.

Sources of quotes and further reading.

A **THE COAST SCENERY OF NORTH DEVON.** E A Newell Arber. J M Dent. 1911. 64 Illustrations. 12 Figs. 261 pages. [Facsimile Edition: Kingsmead Reprints Bath 1969]

B **LIFE AND LETTERS OF R S HAWKER.** C E Byles. Bodley Head. 1905

C **WESTWARD HO!** Charles Kingsley. Macmillan, London. 1855

D **DEVON a new survey of England.** W G Hoskins. Collins, London. 1954

E **OUT OF APPLEDORE.** W J Slade. Conway Maritime Press, London. 1959

F **THE HIDDEN EDGE OF EXMOOR.** David Kester and Elizabeth Webb. Thematic Trails. 2011

G **HARTLAND QUAY the story of a vanished port.** Michael Nix and Mark Myers. Hartland Quay Museum, North Devon. 1982

H **SENSE AND SENSIBILITY.** Jane Austen. 1811

I **STALKY AND CO.** Rudyard Kipling. 1899

J **A BRIEF HISTORY OF WESTWARD HO!** Westward Ho! History Group

K **BUILDINGS OF ENGLAND: North Devon.** Nikolaus Pevsner. 1952

L **TARKA THE OTTER** Henry Williamson. 1927

M **COASTAL MANAGEMENT AND COASTAL EROSION; Westward Ho! and N W Devon 1800-2000.** Chronological notes and index to sources for reference, Thematic Trails 2000

N **SWANAGE: Its history, resources as an invigorating health resort, botany/geology.** Edited by John Braye. William Henry Everett and Son. 1890

O **ILLUSTRATED HISTORY OF APPLEDORE; part 1 and part 2.** David Carter. 2000 & 2009

P **Publications of the North Devon Maritime Museum, Appledore** include:
 APPLEDORE HANDMAIDEN OF THE SEA. John Beara. 1976
 GRENVILLE. Alison Grant 1991
 SALMON NETTING IN NORTH DEVON. Alison Grant and Philip Waters. 1998
 HMS WEAZLE 1782-1799. Bob and Ann Brock. 1998
 NORTHAM BURROWS A mixture of Memories and Facts. Philip Waters. 2005

Acknowledgements

For artwork we thank the following: My late father, Joe Keene, for 'Vicarage Cliffs' (page 7), 'Reefs' (page 47) and 'Johanna' (page 55). A special thanks to Kester Webb for the time and effort spend on-site in measuring and executing 'Speke's Mill Mouth' (page 26). Thanks also to Paul Lewin for the paintings which hang in my lounge and are reminders of a special coast. One of these is reproduced on page 31. A thank you to Michael Lee, who has kindly allowed us to print a copy of his evocative painting of 'Lucy at Bucks Mills' (page 83), and to Jane Koldewey who made a splendid 'bath time' cartoon (page 112) from my simple instructions.

The etching of Blackchurch Rock, 1822, (page 71) comes from the West Country Studies Library collection, Castle Street, Exeter. The painting by Charles Napier Hemy, 'Among the Shingle at Clovelly', 1864, (page 76), is courtesy of the Laing Art Gallery, Tyne and Wear Museums. The painting now catalogued as 'Estuary of the River Taw, Devon' by Thomas Girton, circa 1797, (page 115) is courtesy of the Yale Center for British Art, New Haven, USA.

Photographic support was given in particular by Chris Howes, who against his better judgement kayaked the Hartland coast with me - he capsized only once! I owe all my personal, "me in my kayak" shots on the Hartland coast to Chris: (pages 19, 21, 23, 53, 85). The telephoto shot on page 63 was taken from the shore by Janet Keene. The useful air photo of the Chapman Rocks at low tide (page 61) was taken by Kester Webb.

Thanks go to Justin Seedhouse, National Trust Head Ranger for Bideford Bay and Hartland, for providing a wealth of information on the Embury Beacon site (page 19). The National Trust is a Registered Charity No 205846. Similarly, thanks go to Stephen Hobbs of Hartland who, in correspondence, had a great fund of local information which caused me much thought. Finally, a thank you to Richard Webber who flew the Auster with intuitive skill, judging just what I wanted and tilting and circling at the smallest signal to get the best perspectives. Any locations missed were simply the result of me sometimes not recognising from the air just where we were. The flight was a moving experience.

Lundy midsummer sunset from Westward Ho!

North Devon Thematic Trails

Literature which, through education as a source of pleasure and recreation, aims to increase our understanding, interpretation and appreciation of valued environments. Our principal **North Devon publications** are as follows:

The Hidden Edge of Exmoor
David Kester Webb and Elizabeth Webb (2011) ISBN 978-0-948444-57-9

Classic Landforms of the North Devon Coast
Peter Keene (1986,1996) ISBN 978-0-948444-58-6

Lyn in Flood, Watersmeet to Lynmouth
Peter Keene and Derek Elsom (1990, 2003) ISBN 978-0-948444-20-3

Valley of Rocks, Lynton
Peter Keene and Brian Pearce (1993, 2000) ISBN 978-0948444-25-8

The Cliffs of Saunton
Peter Keene and Chris Cornford (1995) ISBN 978-0-948444-24-1

Braunton Burrows Ecology Trail
Janet Keene (1996, 2003) ISBN 978-0-948444-30-2

Exploring Barnstaple
John Bradbeer (1990, 2002) ISBN 978-0-948444-42-5

Exploring Bideford
Peter Christie (1989, 2000) ISBN 978-0948444-31-9

Northam Burrows Estuary Environments
Janet and Peter Keene (1997) ISBN 978-0-948444-33-3

Westward Ho! Against the Sea
Peter Keene (1986, 1997) ISBN 978-0948444-34-0

The Cliffs of Westward Ho! a sense of time
Peter Keene (2004) ISBN 978-0948444-35-7

Bucks Mills, people and place
John Bradbeer (2011) ISBN 978-0-948444-56-2

The Cliffs of Hartland Quay
Peter Keene (1989, 2006) ISBN 978-0-948444-46-3

Geology at Hartland Quay
Alan Childs and Chris Cornford (1989) ISBN 978-0-948444-12-8

Strawberry Water to Marsland Mouth
Peter Keene (1990) ISBN 978-0-948444-06-7

The North-West Devon Coast, A Celebration of Cliffs and Seashore from the Hartland Peninsula to the Taw-Torridge Estuary. Peter Keene (2013) ISBN 978-0-948444-61-6

This selection of North Devon walks, guides and landscape companions, published by Thematic Trails, may be bought at selected information centres, museums and shops local to sites, or can be obtained directly from Thematic Trails by contacting us at the address below. A fully illustrated catalogue of some 250 publications stocked by Thematic Trails, together with further details of this literature can be inspected by visiting our web site: **www.thematic-trails.org** which also has purchase facilities on-line or by post.

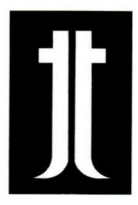

Thematic Trails

7 Norwood Avenue, Kingston Bagpuize, Oxfordshire, OX13 5AD
For advice or information:
Telephone: 01865 820522   or   Email: keene@thematic-trails.org
Thematic Trails is a not-for-profit registered educational charity no 801188